T0183787

SpringerBriefs in Information Systems

Series editor
Jörg Becker

More information about this series at http://www.springer.com/series/10189

D. Laurie Hughes • Yogesh K. Dwivedi
Antonis C. Simintiras • Nripendra P. Rana

Success and Failure of IS/IT Projects

A State of the Art Analysis and Future Directions

 Springer

D. Laurie Hughes
School of Management
Swansea University
Wales, UK

Yogesh K. Dwivedi
School of Management
Swansea University
Wales, UK

Antonis C. Simintiras
Gulf University for Science & Technology

Nripendra P. Rana
School of Management
Swansea University
Wales, UK

ISSN 2192-4929   ISSN 2192-4937   (electronic)
SpringerBriefs in Information Systems
ISBN 978-3-319-22999-7   ISBN 978-3-319-23000-9   (eBook)
DOI 10.1007/978-3-319-23000-9

Library of Congress Control Number: 2015953858

Springer Cham Heidelberg New York Dordrecht London

© The Author(s) 2016
This work is subject to copyright. All rights are reserved by the Publisher, whether the whole or part of the material is concerned, specifically the rights of translation, reprinting, reuse of illustrations, recitation, broadcasting, reproduction on microfilms or in any other physical way, and transmission or information storage and retrieval, electronic adaptation, computer software, or by similar or dissimilar methodology now known or hereafter developed.
The use of general descriptive names, registered names, trademarks, service marks, etc. in this publication does not imply, even in the absence of a specific statement, that such names are exempt from the relevant protective laws and regulations and therefore free for general use.
The publisher, the authors and the editors are safe to assume that the advice and information in this book are believed to be true and accurate at the date of publication. Neither the publisher nor the authors or the editors give a warranty, express or implied, with respect to the material contained herein or for any errors or omissions that may have been made.

Printed on acid-free paper

Springer International Publishing AG Switzerland is part of Springer Science+Business Media (www.springer.com)

*To Beth for her never-ending support
and belief in me. To my children Oliver,
Ewan, Cerys, and Llewelyn of whom
I'm so proud.*

Laurie Hughes

*To Professor Andrew Henley—a gentleman
who has imparted his invaluable guidance
and support to me in my career development.
In my experience, his commitment to his staff
is second to none; he always gives his best
to nurture and encourage them. I owe
a great debt of gratitude to Professor Henley.*

Yogesh K. Dwivedi

To my wife Mary and our son Constantine.

Antonis C. Simintiras

*To my wife, Vijeyta, and my adorable
daughter, Shambhavi.*

Nripendra P. Rana

Foreword

I am pleased to provide a foreword to this book. For over 60 years, computers and information technologies have helped organizations improve their business processes and delivery of products and services. There is a now a large body of work on what firms must do to get their IS/IT projects right. The advice is, more often than not, based on sound logic, and thus, they have formed the basis for how organizations plan, design, and implement projects of different sizes and complexity. IS/IT projects have also progressively become important drivers of organizational strategy and they offer firms a lot more than operational efficiencies. They can, indeed, have a transformational impact on how businesses gather real-time intelligence, access markets, and develop stronger customer relationships.

It is perhaps inevitable that a proportion of IS/IT projects will continue to fail. The inherent complexities of implementing such projects, especially the social and cultural dimensions, can overwhelm managers even when they have the best project management tools at their disposal. How can managers improve their chances of implementing IS/IT projects? What does academic scholarship have to offer organizations in this context? How can managers blend formal project management approaches with the more difficult task of getting people committed to a project? This book squarely addresses such questions and provides a rigorous but very readable analysis of IS/IT project success and failure.

The authors have done a commendable job of synthesizing key insights from published research and they provide an excellent analysis of IS/IT project success and failure. It is especially heartening that the analysis is not merely explanatory. The implications of academic research for practicing managers are clearly and explicitly spelt out at the end of chapters. Overall, both the serious scholar and the practitioner will find this book interesting and relevant. I very much welcome this important addition to the extant literature on IS/IT projects and hope that the book will be well received.

School of Business and Economics   M.N. Ravishankar, M.D.
Loughborough University
Loughborough, UK
M.N.Ravishankar@lboro.ac.uk

About the Author

Dr. M.N. Ravishankar is Professor of Globalisation and Emerging Markets and Head of International Business, Strategy and Innovation at the School of Business and Economics, Loughborough University, UK. His research interests span cultural conflicts in the implementation of strategy, offshore outsourcing of work, and digitally enabled transformations in emerging markets. His research articles have been published in journals such as Information Systems Research, Journal of Information Technology, Information Systems Journal, European Journal of Information Systems, Omega, and Journal of Vocational Behaviour.

Foreword

IS Project failure has been widely researched, discussed, and debated for over four decades, but frustratingly the industry is still unable to deliver consistent successful outcomes (Nelson 2007; Dwivedi et al. 2013, 2015). The effects of IS failure are huge and the costs to the organization concerned can be disastrous. If the IS industry was instead a manufacturer of vehicles or a builder of houses, such a track record would be catastrophic.

Academics have analyzed the failure of IS projects attempting to identify root causes and contributory factors. Studies have shown that projects are complex and difficult to manage and fail due to a multitude of factors (Pinto and Mantel 1990), often exhibiting no single root cause (Janssen et al. 2015). Why is it that failure seems a continuous theme? Have academics not communicated the key underlying issues, and if they have, is industry not listening? Why is practice making the same failures over and over again? Is research solving the wrong problem? Is the teaching and associated curriculums not suitable for improving the situation? Is the practitioner and academic gap too wide for meaningful change? These are all valid and relevant questions and ones that need to be explored continuously until we can significantly reduce project failure.

This book presents the key topics from the IS failure literature and provides an analysis of the critical factors behind project success exploring how success is judged by different stakeholders. As an IS community we still have trouble defining success and have difficulty highlighting what success really looks like.

Project managers have been criticized for their lack of soft skills and overemphasis on the technical deliverables. These topics are discussed in this book and the merits of a people-centered approach to project management are explored. This theme is developed further in later sections in the book from the perspective of the closer integration of change and project management where the merits and issues are examined.

The ongoing academic examination of IS project performance is of utmost importance to ensure we can facilitate a change in outcomes. We need to explore new avenues and find ways to communicate the required key messages effectively not just to our peer group but to industry as whole. Only time will tell if Henry Ford's statement will still ring true in years to come "*if you always do what you have always done…*" you know the rest.

Delft, The Netherlands   Marijn Janssen, M.D.

References

Dwivedi Y, Wastell D, Laumer S, Henriksen HZ, Myers MD, Bunker D, Elbanna A, Ravishankar MN and Srivastava SC (2015) Research on information systems failures and successes: status update and future directions. Inf Syst Front 17(1): 143–157

Dwivedi YK, Henriksen HZ, Wastell D, De R (2011) Grand successes and failures in IT: public and private sectors. Springer, New York, pp 670

Janssen M, Van der Voort H, Van Veenstra AFE (2015) Failure of large transformation projects from the viewpoint of complex adaptive systems: management principles for dealing with project dynamics. Inf Syst Front (ISF) 17(1):15–29

Nelson RR (2007) IT project management: infamous failures, classic mistakes and best practices. MISQ Exec 6(2):67–78

Pinto JK, Mantel SJ (1990) The causes of project failure. IEEE Trans Eng Manage 37(4): 269–276

About the Author

Prof. Dr. Marijn Janssen is full Professor in ICT and Governance and Head of the Information and Communication Technology section of the Technology, Policy and Management Faculty of Delft University of Technology. He worked for the Ministry of Justice and was involved in large transformation projects. He was involved in EU-funded projects in the past (a.o. EGovRTD2020, eGovPoliNet and Engage), is co-editor-in-chief of Government Information Quarterly, is associate editor of the International Journal of Electronic Business Research (IJEBR), Electronic Journal of eGovernment (EJEG), and International Journal of E-Government Research (IJEGR), is conference chair of IFIP EGOV2015 and IFIP I3E2015 conference (about big and open data innovation), and is chairing mini-tracks at the DG.o, ICEGOV, HICCS, and AMCIS conferences. His research interests are in the field of orchestration, (shared) services, intermediaries, open and big data, and infrastructures within constellations of public and private organizations. He was ranked as one of the leading e-government researchers in a survey in 2009 and 2014 and published over 320 refereed publications. More information: www.tbm.tudelft.nl/marijnj.

Preface

The dismal track record of organization's inability to deliver successful Information System (IS) projects has been a matter of public record for decades. What is most frustrating about this is that it keeps happening time and time again. The phrase *large government IT project* can have many connotations, depending on who the commentator is, but to most people, even industry outsiders, the phrase evokes a familiar response: *failure*. It is not just government projects that have this problem; numerous projects from across many industries have suffered the effects of failure resulting in catastrophic problems for the organizations concerned.

The reasons behind the inability of organizations to deliver consistently successful IS projects are multifaceted. There is no tangible single cause of failure, no individual root cause that can be highlighted as the key fundamental problem that affects all projects. Projects fail due to poor project management, insufficient focus on change management issues, mismanagement of requirements, ineffective project sponsorship, poor business case, and so on. Most startling from this track record of poor delivery is the inability of the industry as a whole to learn the lessons of past mistakes. Time and time again we see the same root causes of failure and the resulting fallout in terms of the effects on the organization or the claim and counter claim in the civil courts over who was ultimately responsible. *How did we get here*? This is a good question but a better one is—*what lessons can we learn from analyzing past failures that can help us deliver consistent successful projects in the future*? This is covered in the subsequent chapters and it is a topic that academics must not lose focus on to effect a change in outcomes.

Organizations can deliver IS projects successfully. Studies have empirically analyzed the components of successful projects and many have developed a set of Critical Success Factors (CSF) that have been positioned as a form of checklist to follow in order to mitigate failure. It is not clear from the literature if the documented instances of failed projects have attempted to adhere to an agreed set of CSFs or if factors outside of these were to blame for the projects' demise. Academic studies have produced a number of widely cited CSF-based frameworks that seem to cover the traditional technical areas of delivery as well as the stakeholder focused factors relating to adoption and realization of more longer term benefits. However, these success-orientated frameworks do not figure in the practitioner guidance or bodies of knowledge. Therefore, leading one to conclude that at best, there exists an informal and somewhat haphazard relationship between academics and industry, or it signifies a perceived lack of relevance and influence from academic circles. The benefit of bringing the two sides closer together is a subject covered in this book.

The last 10 years or more have seen a significant push from industry and governance bodies to professionalize project management practitioners and key project staff. However, there is no evidence to support that this has resulted in any significant change in project outcomes, especially in the context of large IS projects. This is a staggering fact and one that should greatly trouble many organizations about to embark on a major IS project. The association between success and the links to practitioner training and the use of project management methods is an underresearched area and a somewhat surprising fact given the significant investment in standards and training.

This book outlines the criticism of project managers for their lack of *people* or so-called *soft* skills, as historically the profession has been preoccupied with delivering to the parameters of time, cost, and quality. The emergence of change management as a distinct profession with its own governance, practitioner status, and bodies of knowledge perhaps highlights the inability of the project management profession to adequately address the people side of project delivery. It is too early to fully quantify the impact of change management on the IS industry as a whole and its ability to deliver more consistent successful projects, as the academic literature has yet to fully address this topic. However, the recognition of the part played in the application of soft skills and focus on the people side of projects is widely referenced in the literature.

From the organizational perspective, the application of both change and project management can be somewhat confusing in that the de facto standards do not fully address how both disciplines should work together. *When is the best time to initiate change management? How can I identify how much change management resource I need and how do I know if its value for money?* These are pertinent questions and subjects that are addressed in this book as we explore the evolving landscape of projects and the closer integration of change and project management.

Success and Failure of IS/IT Projects: A State-of-the-Art Analysis and Future Directions is a book that provides the reader with a full outline of the key issues surrounding the delivery of IS projects and the inherent complexities. The reader is guided through key areas from current literature and the main topics are discussed and debated in their relevant context. The core problems facing the IS industry are tackled head on and omissions in knowledge and research are highlighted where they are relevant. The continued academic study of this topic is vital in order to influence and facilitate change. This book is positioned as an important advance in this process.

Wales, UK

D. Laurie Hughes
Yogesh K. Dwivedi
Antonis C. Simintiras
Nripendra P. Rana

Contents

Chapter 1
Introduction

The failure of Information Systems (IS) projects has been a constant theme for the last 40 years or more with the loss of many millions of pounds for the organizations concerned (Dwivedi et al. 2013a, 2015a, b). Despite attempts to professionalize the industry with the adoption of formal structured project management methodologies, bodies of knowledge, IS development methods and processes, formal major project gateway reviews, and professional practitioner certification, project failure is still a regular occurrence. The widely cited CHAOS report (Standish Group 2013) highlighted a trend of IS success rates of between 29 and 39 % for the period 2004–2012. This suggests that while success rates are improving, well over half of IS projects do not succeed. The 2014 National Audit Office's (NAO) report on the failed BBC Digital Media Initiative (DMI) project reminds us that large IS failure remains an ever-present issue. The NAO highlighted a number of factors that were responsible for the £125.9 million project abandonment, including lack of BBC executive scrutiny, no individual senior staff member acting as the single point of accountability, and poor reporting arrangements that were not fit for purpose (BBC 2014). The IS sector is under greater scrutiny than ever before, with executives being all too aware that historical failures have had a dramatic effect on the organizations concerned, both in terms of huge financial cost and business sustainability from the impact of failure (Avison and Wilson 2002; Beynon-Davies 1995; Gauld 2007; McGrath 2002; Mitev 1996; Pan et al. 2008). The continual academic review of project performance within the IS industry is of vital importance until such time the sector can demonstrate step changes in consistently delivering successful outcomes.

The issues of the historical focus of project management predominantly delivering to the defined technical elements of time, cost, and quality have led to a greater emphasis on stakeholder satisfaction criteria in the development of project success factors Atkinson 1999; Cooke-Davies 2002; Fortune and White 2006; Dwivedi et al. 2015b; Hyvari 2006; Müller and Judgev 2012; Turner 2009). Industry-based studies have identified that projects perform poorly where users lack involvement and that user participation has a major effect on successful outcomes (Standish Group 2013).

© The Author(s) 2016
D.L. Hughes et al., *Success and Failure of IS/IT Projects*,
SpringerBriefs in Information Systems, DOI 10.1007/978-3-319-23000-9_1

This increased focus on stakeholder satisfaction has led to greater scrutiny of project manager performance in their application of so-called *soft* skills to complement the traditional project management capability (Esa and Samad 2014) and deliver more consistent successful outcomes. However, studies have highlighted that as a group, project managers have only moderate skills to manage users and their expectations (Standish Group 2013), which perhaps is a reflection of the technical emphasis within practitioner training.

Change management has emerged as a distinct discipline with its own standards, numerous models and frameworks, and an active academic community. Change initiatives (projects) where good change management practices are implemented can increase the probability of successful organizational change by a factor of four (Change Management Institute 2013). The tasks of leading and sustaining change can be complex and often entail the interplay of multiple factors involving action by people at every level of the business (Buchanan et al. 2005; Pettigrew and Whipp 1993). The closer integration of both project and change management is advocated in some of the practitioner guidance (Prosci 2012) and academic literature (Hornstein 2015; Parker et al. 2013). However, the challenge of moving from a current position of separate methodologies, different standards bodies, and in some cases totally separate internal organizational structures is a step change for many organizations but has the potential to offer a greater chance of project success.

The main purpose of this book is to set out a contributing narrative to the discussion and debate of IS project failure and project success via a thorough analysis of the current literature and the identification of omissions in academic knowledge and practitioner guidance. This book will be of value to academics requiring an understanding of the key aspects of IS project delivery and those who have knowledge of specific areas of change or project management that need more detailed knowledge of either subject. Practitioners may also benefit from key aspects of the text, in particular the causes of project failure, components of project success, and the closer integration of change and project management.

The remaining sections of the book are outlined as follows:

Chapter 2—Analyzes and discusses the key components and causes of project failure from the literature and develops each of the main topics from the project management and people-related perspectives.

Chapter 3—Reviews the classification and varying perspectives of project success and the key critical success factors from the literature, in particular the factors surrounding project management and the role of the sponsor.

Chapter 4—Discusses the processes and practice associated with project management and the practical aspects of methodology and project delivery.

Chapter 5—Examines the key components and processes of change management and the issues of resistance and adoption.

Chapter 6—Develops the case for the closer integration of change and project management and details the practical implications for each of the presented options.

Chapter 7—Provides concluding remarks and summary of key points.

Chapter 2
Project Failure and Its Contributing Factors

Although studies have attempted to articulate an accepted theory of IS failure, the literature has demonstrated many alternative views of definition and causes. What is clear is that the failure of systems is complex and multifaceted. Failure itself can have many levels, in that a project can be an outright failure and abandoned or is delivered to specification but does not meet the needs of stakeholders. Each of these instances can be viewed as a failed project but may have different underlying causes and categories of failure. The traditional performance-oriented measures of failure, namely, time cost and quality, only provide a limited set of criteria, failing to include any stakeholder usage aspects. The key measure of failure is whether the system receives sufficient support for it to continue to exist (Sauer 1993); without this the project is a certain failure.

This section starts with highlighting the key issues in the classification of project failure in that failure has many facets and is subject to different perceptions depending on the stakeholder type. The subsequent subsections move on to the presentation of a taxonomy of project failure highlighting the main causes from the body of literature. Each of the main failure types is grouped into a category of project management (often termed—*technical factors*) or people-related failure to provide some structure to the taxonomy and highlight the key related factors. The section ends with a discussion and analysis of the key failure factors and a summary of the main points.

2.1 Classification of Project Failure

The examination and categorization of project failure has been the subject of extensive study (Flowers 1997; Lyytinen and Hirschheim 1987; Pinto and Mantel 1990; Sauer 1993) with researchers attempting to develop a model or framework that assists with the explanation of project failure. The historical and somewhat traditional measure of project success, namely, time, cost, and quality (Sauer 1993), does not provide

© The Author(s) 2016
D.L. Hughes et al., *Success and Failure of IS/IT Projects*,
SpringerBriefs in Information Systems, DOI 10.1007/978-3-319-23000-9_2

a firm basis to define whether a project is a success or a failure, as it measures the project management or so-called technical elements only. The definition of project failure can be further complicated by how a system can be received by various stakeholder groups. The extensively publicized London Ambulance Service Computer Aided Dispatch (LASCAD) project did not fail in the strict technical sense but failed to meet the expectations of many of the stakeholder groups on the project (Beynon-Davies 1995; Fitzgerald and Russo 2005; McGrath 2002). A system implementation that exceeds its budget, is delivered late, and omits some functionality could be labeled a failure in the strict technical sense as the project has failed to realize many of its defined benefits. But if the same system was embraced by key stakeholders and continued to be used post-implementation delivering significant benefits to the business, would it still be classed as a failure? This alternative view of defining failure from the project management and stakeholder perspectives is covered in Kerzner (2013) where the concept of the customer receiving the *desired value* from the project is discussed, highlighting that failure should be linked to stakeholders not receiving the defined value or benefits from the project.

Projects can be subject to grades of failure. The CHAOS report (Standish Group 2013) defines a category of *challenged* or *impaired* to define a project that has not suffered complete failure but was delivered late, over budget, or failed to deliver the required levels of functionality. The report defines complete failure as those projects that were canceled prior to completion or delivered and never used. The CHAOS report defines project success as those projects that are delivered on time, on budget with required features and functions. Interestingly, these success criteria focus predominantly on the technical deliverables and fail to include any user adoption aspects of project delivery, thereby ignoring the LASCAD study findings in Beynon-Davies (1995), Fitzgerald and Russo (2005), and McGrath (2002), which are fundamental to overall project success. The CHAOS figures have been criticized in some studies (Emam and Koru 2008; Glass 2005) for not identifying the underlying methodology behind the data, resulting in researchers questioning the Standish Group findings.

The classification of project failure can be based on a wide range of factors: poor project management, ineffective project executive, high levels of user resistance, poor change management, changing requirements, and poor planning (Dwivedi et al. 2013a; 2015a, b). Many of these failure factors on their own may not cause the project to fail, but often a project's ultimate demise may be due to a combination of failure factors (Pinto and Mantel 1990). Organizations have continually failed to reap the benefits of the analysis and categorization of project failure, by not performing, or poorly implementing a postmortem process, failing to learn from past mistakes, or conducting post-project reviews for successful projects only (Ewusi-Mensah and Przasnyski 1995; Jones 2006; Verner et al. 2008). This practice of hiding from failure has resulted in many organizations repeating the same mistakes or engendering a culture where project staff are extremely reluctant to report bad news leading to a continuation of the project failure cycle (Park et al. 2009). Some studies highlight the benefits of failure (Scott and Vessey 2000; Sitkin 1992) and hypothesize that the process of failure can enable organizations to reap the long-term benefits of success through short-term failure. This approach seems pragmatic in the cool light of day, but in the heat of the project engine room, failure is not something a project manager wants to embrace, especially if his or her career depends on delivering a successful project.

The academic analysis of project failure has been an active research area with many authors attempting to provide a definitive classification of failure and its various notions. Lyytinen and Hirschheim (1987) argued that most studies focusing on project failure are based on a largely unarticulated failure concept and defined four major categories of failure from the literature:

- *Correspondence failure*—the system does not meet all of its goals and quality criteria and the implemented system does not correspond to the requirements.
- *Process failure*—the system has either not been delivered or has been delivered but has failed to meet its defined criteria in terms of time, budgetary constraints, and schedule.
- *Interaction failure*—the delivered system fails to be adopted by stakeholders or is not used as envisaged, therefore failing to meet the specific benefits of the project.
- *Expectation failure*—the system does not meet the specific needs and expectations of stakeholder groups.

Sauer (1993) highlighted the lack of evidence of a decline in the failure rate of IS projects and developed a *triangle of dependencies* model that supported the notion that a system is not a failure unless stakeholder support for the system ends. Ewusi-Mensah (2003) described abandonment and partial abandonment from the software development project perspective. The study reaffirmed findings from previous research that software systems' failures are the result of human errors in design and are not the consequence of material failure. Flowers (1997) identified a number of common factors associated with project failure and proposed that a system can be defined as having failed where performance is suboptimal and the system does not operate as expected, the system is rejected by users or performance is not as specified, where costs outweigh the actual benefits, and where a system is abandoned before completion. The difficulties faced by researchers and practitioners in the definition of project failure are highlighted in Pinto and Mantel (1990) where the study proposed that success and failure cannot be judged on one measure but must be assessed based on several criteria. Projects can be viewed as a failure in one organization but deemed a success in another—it is a question of perspective and judgment (Dwivedi et al. 2015b; Pinto and Mantel 1990) and highlights the complexity of defining project success and failure within a stakeholder and organizational context. Identifying and classifying project failure within a single organization is problematic; especially in cases where a dominant sponsor articulates a positive, biased narrative to give a better account of a dysfunctional and problematic system as highlighted in Bartis and Mitev (2008).

Attempting to classify project failure with an industry-wide model or set of criteria still eludes academics, and although general frameworks and models such as those listed in Lyytinen and Hirschheim (1987) and Sauer (1993) can assist practitioners and project executives, the multiplicity of criteria such as those listed in Pinto and Mantel (1990) highlights the difficulties in defining a *one-size-fits-all* model to measure project outcomes.

2.2 Taxonomy of the Key Factors Associated with Project Failure

Previous studies have highlighted and categorized the key failure factors that have been identified from IS failure research and have attempted to provide structure and insight into the main causes of project failure. Some theoretical studies present a model or framework that aims to help organizations understand and take steps to avoid IS failure (Bronte-Stuart 2009; Davis et al. 1992; Goulielmos 2005; Heeks 2002; Keider 1974; Nelson 2007; Poulymenakou and Holmes 1996). Other theoretical studies have focused on key elements or specific factors of project failure relating to project management, leadership, or human nontechnical factors (Ewusi-Mensah 2003; Lin and Pan 2011; Nixon et al. 2012; Perkins 2006; Young 2005). A taxonomy of IS project failure is presented in some studies (Al-Ahmad and Al-Fagih 2009; Dwivedi et al. 2013b; Fenech and Raffaele 2013) by highlighting commonly occurring failure factors that organizations should focus on in an attempt to reduce IS failure. The literature highlights the undeniable fact that organizations do not learn from failure and are unable/unwilling to change, highlighting a pattern of repeating the same mistakes time after time (Lyytinen and Robey 1999).

Project failure studies that contain an empirical element to the research (Bartis and Mitev 2008; Brown and Jones 1998; Bussen and Myers 1997), or focus on the case study of a specific project failure (Barker and Frolick 2003; Beynon-Davies 1995; Gauld 2007), form the basis for the main analysis of the taxonomy presented in Table 2.1. Each of the research papers has been reviewed to extract the relevant factors and salient points associated with specific references to project failure. The taxonomy highlights the list of identified failure factors and the associated references for each. The failure factors have been separated into two main high-level groups: *Project Management* factors (also termed *technical* factors) and *People-related* factors. The project management factors include the factors associated with the traditional project management tasks and processes such as requirements management, risk management, planning, budget management, and task management. The *People-related* factors include the so-called *soft* factors that have a stakeholder or user bias and are not generally aligned with the traditional concepts of project management deliverables. This grouping includes change management-related issues, user resistance, system adoption, and executive engagement activities. The selected groupings of failure factors reflects an attempt to highlight some of the issues within the project or change management sphere of influence that can be exposed to address some of the underlying causes. References may appear in more than one category of failure; this reflects the fact that studies have highlighted a number of factors that have jointly contributed to the overall project failure.

The following subsections discuss the key themes from the taxonomy of project failure listed in Table 2.1 under their *project management* or *people-related* headings. Associated factors are grouped together under an overall theme heading to provide clarity.

Table 2.1 Categorized failure factors

IS failure factor	References	PM factor	People factor
Poor requirements management	Bussen and Myers (1997), Emam and Koru (2008), Gauld (2007), Keil et al. (1998), Nawi et al. (2011), Pan et al. (2008), Rob (2003), Schmidt et al. (2001), Standing et al. (2006), Verner and Abdullah (2012)	✓	
Poor project management and project planning	Avison and Wilson (2002), Brown and Jones (1998), Emam and Koru (2008), Gauld (2007), Jones (2006), Keil et al. (1998), Nawi et al. (2011), Pan et al. (2008), Philip et al. (2009), Standing et al. (2006), Tukel and Rom (1998), Verner et al. (2008), Verner and Abdullah (2012), Wallace et al. (2004), Yeo (2002)	✓	
Scale and complexity of project	Nawi et al. (2011), Scott and Vessey (2000), Standish Group (2013), Verner and Abdullah (2012), Wallace et al. (2004)	✓	
Poor budget and risk management	Conboy (2010), Jones (2006), Keil et al. (1998), Pan et al. (2008), Verner et al. (2008)	✓	
Poor business case, and evaluation process	Barker and Frolick (2003), Pan et al. (2008), Sauer et al. (1997), Standing et al. (2006)	✓	
Inadequate management structure and support	Avison and Wilson (2002), Philip et al. (2009)	✓	
Inadequate postmortem process	Ewusi-Mensah and Przasnyski (1995), Jones (2006), Verner et al. (2008)	✓	
Poor change management and user resistance	Attarzadeh and Ow (2008), Barker and Frolick (2003), Bartis and Mitev (2008), Beynon-Davies (1995), Brown and Jones (1998), Bussen and Myers (1997), Fitzgerald and Russo (2005), Gauld (2007), Hirschheim and Newman (1988), Keil et al. (1998), Klaus and Blanton (2010), Lemon et al. (2002), McGrath (2002), Mitev (1996), Pan et al. (2008), Newman and Sabherwal (1996), Philip et al. (2009), Rob (2003), Schmidt et al. (2001), Scott and Vessey (2000), Standing et al. (2006), Yeo (2002), Warne and Hart (1997), Winklhofer (2001)		✓
Poor executive support and sponsorship for project	Bussen and Myers (1997), Emam and Koru (2008), Keil et al. (1998), Lemon et al. (2002), Nawi et al. (2011), Pan et al. (2008), Schmidt et al. (2001), Standing et al. (2006)		✓
Poor contractor and stakeholder relationship	Brown and Jones (1998), Nawi et al. (2011), Pan et al. (2008), Verner and Abdullah (2012), Warne and Hart (1997), Yeo (2002)		✓
Lack of staff commitment, motivation, performance, and turnover issues	Bussen and Myers (1997), Conway and Limayem (2011), Linberg (1999), Newman and Sabherwal (1996), Rob (2003), Verner et al. (2008)		✓

2.3   Project Management-Related Failure Factors

The grouping of failure factors in this section is as follows:

- Poor requirements management
- Poor project management and project planning
- Scale and complexity of project
- Poor risk and budget management
- Poor business case and evaluation process
- Inadequate management structure and support
- Inadequate postmortem process

2.3.1   Poor Requirements Management

The definition and subsequent management of project requirements together with project specification are frequent factors in the reasons cited for project failure. Studies relying on feedback from project managers and IT departments (Emam and Koru 2008; Keil et al. 1998; Schmidt et al. 2001), cite the misunderstanding and subsequent change in requirements and specification as significant risk factors in IS development projects. Projects that suffer from inadequate and unclear requirements highlight the significant impact on organizations when projects do not manage these aspects effectively (Bussen and Myers 1997; Nawi et al. 2011; Pan et al. 2008). Projects that have failed due to poor management of specification (Rob 2003; Standing et al. 2006; Verner and Abdullah 2012) describe failure in the context of poor requirements management. The case of the BSkyB CRM project as outlined in Verner and Abdullah (2012) identified a project that failed to deliver its intended benefits and resulted in a 5-year legal battle between BSkyB and the system integrator EDS. The study findings highlight the main reasons for failure as inadequate and unclear requirements, poor project scope, and a contractor that lacked the required skills to complete the project. The reliance on consultant/contractors to solicit the requirements gathering process can be problematic if not managed properly as highlighted in Brown and Jones (1998), where a failed HISS project suffered from staff feeling intimidated by the external consultants. The study highlighted that users did not fully understand the processes or technical language employed to facilitate requirements and gain acceptance of key design aspects (Brown and Jones 1998).

The control and configuration of requirements is a key project task and the successful management of this aspect can mitigate any scope creep risks, ensuring timescales and budgets are maintained. Changes to requirements should be seen as business as usual on most projects, but the project manager must ensure that each change follows a structured management process where the impact of any change is formally assessed in terms of cost and timescale and its affect on the remainder of the project schedule. Best practice in these areas is covered in the main project management standards such as Project Management Body of Knowledge (PMBoK®)

and Projects in Controlled Environments (PRINCE2®). However, the studies that have cited poor, unclear, and inadequate requirements as reasons for failure (Bussen and Myers 1997; Nawi et al. 2011; Pan et al. 2008) highlight a separate issue, in that the definition of requirements, especially in the context of large projects, is problematic. This issue is further compounded by long lead-time projects where the business processes may have changed or evolved since the initial requirements definition. The net effect of these circumstances is a project that is scheduled to deliver an out-of-date, irrelevant system that fails to meet the organizations needs. Additionally, the expectation that users should be able to define a detailed requirements specification for a large complex system as an early life-cycle activity is a *big ask* for any organization stakeholder group. The adoption of a Sitkin-style approach (Sitkin 1992) to requirements management, where it is accepted that failure forms part of the learning process, seems to be an approach that could yield benefits but could be a *difficult sell* for many cost conscious project executives. Further academic study to fully investigate the unrealistic expectations of developing an up-front detailed set of requirements for a large complex system could help to inform organizations of the pitfalls of this approach.

2.3.2   Poor Project Management and Project Planning

Although limited by the restricted participant group, surveys of IS professionals including project managers and project executives provide some insight into the problems faced by practitioners and the wider stakeholder community in the delivery of projects. Via a study looking at the views of IS practitioners from 70 separate projects, Verner et al. (2008) identified that most of the failed projects had problems with poor project management and planning issues. In a study that surveyed the feedback from respondents who had experienced IS project failure, Yeo (2002) highlighted that a significant proportion of problems related to project planning. Comparable studies (Emam and Koru 2008; Keil et al. 1998; Standing et al. 2006) highlight that poor project management exacerbated the problems within the project, and in terms of top reasons for project failure, poor project management was viewed as one of the top five. Project management failings are often highlighted when large public sector and health-related projects fail. Nawi et al. (2011) cited project management planning processes as key failure factors within Malaysian public sector projects. Philip et al. (2009) cited project management immaturity between client and vendors as a key failure factor within offshore development projects. Jones (2004) concluded that project management was the overriding factor across all common problems that can influence success or failure. Studies highlight the fact that ill-planned and poorly managed, large and multifaceted projects (Gauld 2007) are more likely to fail, as are large projects that are managed by an inexperienced project manager (Pan et al. 2008).

Studies citing poor project management as one of the reasons for failure generally suffer from a lack of detail as to what aspects of project management have been the contributory factor. It is not clear from the literature if the failings are methodology based or personal attributes such as style, or the approach of the individual project manager. This omission within the literature highlights a number of key gaps in the academic analysis of project manager performance and is one that could be of benefit to the overall understanding of project failure. Avots (1969) identified that projects suffered from the lack of a *fit-for-purpose* project management methodology, but the study included non-technology-based genres of projects. Al-Ahmad and Al-Fagih (2009) developed a taxonomy of the root causes of project failure and highlighted that a key finding was that most of the symptoms of failure can be aligned with the project management root cause. However, their study failed to provide the necessary detail to fully explain the assertion. Other project failures attributed to project management causes are more clear cut; the failure of Australian telecoms company One.Tel in 2001 as studied by Avison and Wilson (2002) highlights that a lack of controls and formal development methodology caused many problems within the organization. This ultimately led to the failure of the billing system and subsequent collapse of the company. However, what is not clear from the study is whether the project manager was a contributory factor, or if the organization's lack of adoption of a formal methodology was the root cause. In a study analyzing project failure at NASA, Sauser et al. (2009) hypothesized that ascertaining if the project management was good or bad was the wrong approach. Instead he posed the question: *was it the right management for the situation, the task and the environment?* Sauser highlighted that just because something works well in one situation does not necessarily mean it will work in another and analyzed the situational fit of different project management styles. Project managers are confronted by projects that are becoming increasingly multifaceted involving stakeholders with diverse interests, fast changing technologies, and distributed knowledge bases. The modern project manager requires a multiskilled set of attributes and adaptable management style to steer a path through to successful outcomes (Söderlund 2011).

Many of the case studies that investigate project failure omit to highlight the specific project management methodology used within the organization (Barker and Frolick 2003; Bartis and Mitev 2008; Hirschheim and Newman 1988; Lehtinen et al. 2014; Mitev 1996; Pan et al. 2008). Other studies fail to identify the project management methodology but hint that one existed (Gauld 2007; Newman and Sabherwal 1996; Verner and Abdullah 2012). However, many of these studies concede that the methodology was either not implemented correctly or applied ineffectively. The studies that explicitly state the methodology used (Beynon-Davies 1995; Scott and Vessey 2000) highlight the fact that unless the organization incorporates all the other measures required to mitigate project failure, the adoption of a project management methodology in isolation will not guarantee success. Organizations seem to continue applying the same methodology as previous projects or are mandated to do so via public sector procurement rules, yet fail to analyze the suitability of the methods used or how to apply the methodology differently to yield a different outcome. The lack of academic focus on the suitability, benefits, and limitations of specific project management standards and methodologies is a core area in need of further research.

2.3.3 Scale and Complexity of Project

Large-scale industry surveys and project failure case studies support the fact that the IS sector has a very poor record of delivering large and complex projects over a number of decades. Results show that very few large projects perform well in the context of time, cost, and scope and are ten times more likely to fail outright than smaller and less complex projects (Standish Group 2013). This trend is supported by specific case studies where the size and complexity issues are stated as being significant or contributory factors in the failure of projects. It is difficult to fully establish from the literature if project scale and complexity are key issues in their own right, or by virtue of a project being large and complex, that additional risk factors apply and the project needs to be managed in a different way. Studies that have analyzed large project failures (Gauld 2007; Jones 2004, 2006; Mitev 1996; Nawi et al. 2011; Verner and Abdullah 2012) highlight the deficiencies from a scale and complexity perspective and identify some of the classic large project failure issues: insufficient resources allocated to user adoption, inadequate project governance, high levels of complexity and integration, and inability of users to fully understand the complexities of the system.

Studies such as Scott and Vessey (2000) highlight the difficulties in managing strategic ERP implementations and propose that large-scale projects are an exercise in organizational learning and that, due to their complexity, failure at some level is inevitable. The recommendation to manage large projects in a different way is made by Jones (2006), who advocates a different approach to the management of risk in the context of large-scale software projects. However, studies that have analyzed a range of large IS project failure case histories (Nelson 2007) highlight that other than size, the projects have little in common. The case against attempting large-scale IS projects has been made by some studies (Standish Group 2013), where the findings question the need for larger projects to exist. Organizations can break up a large project to create a number of individual smaller projects that can be run in parallel, each having the potential to deliver tangible benefits in their own right. But without the proper controls, methodology, and organizational support, successful outcomes are still not certain. Large projects can suffer from project sponsors and management having *blind faith* that success will be achieved as huge amounts of money, resource, and reputations are at stake. In cases such as these, early warning signs are often ignored and the collective belief has the tendency to drown out any dissent from the project staff (Kerzner 2013).

2.3.4 Poor Risk and Budget Management

Risk in the project context is a measure of the probability and consequence of not achieving a defined project outcome or deliverable (Kerzner 2013). This is normally assessed in terms of its probability of occurring and the impact on the project if the risk were to materialize. Project management guidance such as PRojects In Controlled Environments (PRINCE2®) and Project Management Body of Knowledge (PMBoK®) highlight the importance of defining a strategy for the management of risk and for this to be established early in the project and continually addressed throughout the duration of the project. Projects failing due to contributory factors such as poor risk management or budget and estimation issues are ranked highly in studies involving surveys and questionnaires from IS organizations and practitioners (Jones 2004; Tukel and Rom 1998; Verner et al. 2008; Wallace et al. 2004). The study carried out by Verner et al. (2008) surveyed failure from the practitioner perspective, highlighting that risks were not reassessed, controlled, or managed through the project. Keil et al. (1998) theorized whether the high failure rate of IS projects could be due to managers not taking prudent measures to assess and manage the risk on their projects. Successive organizations over many decades seem to have fundamentally failed to effectively identify or manage the risks that have contributed to the failure of their projects. The literature is not clear on whether this is a process issue or a management problem subsequent to risk identification.

Projects that suffer from inaccurate estimation, poor budget management, and status reporting (Jones 2004; Pan et al. 2008) highlight the importance of project managers controlling these aspects of the project and the impact on outcomes if they do not control these areas effectively. Conboy (2010) highlighted the lack of focus on budget setting and budget control in the existing research and questioned this lack of focus within IS development projects. The study analyzed projects within a multinational organization and identified a culture of poor cost control management across all the participant projects, a high tolerance for interim budget deviations, poor control of budget line items, and that budget-related communication was largely nonexistent (Conboy 2010).

2.3.5 Poor Business Case and Evaluation Process

The development of the business case and the identification of the benefits the project will realize are a vital part of modern formal project management standards such as PRINCE2® and PMBoK®. This is an early stage activity and is normally owned by the sponsor (or equivalent) on behalf of the executive. Projects that fail to fully define a clear business case at the onset of the project or omit to revisit the business justification at the end of each stage risk delivering a project with unclear benefits and justification. Studies that reference projects where imprecise objectives and unclear business benefits are identified as failure factors highlight the impact of not developing a sound business case with a realistic benefits management process (Sauer et al. 1997; Standing et al. 2006; Ward and Elvin 1999). The net effect of not creating and agreeing a fully functioning business case is a project with an increased risk of potential problems further on in the project lifecycle.

The implementation-based studies of Barker and Frolick (2003) and Pan et al. (2008) highlight instances where organizations have either chosen not to undertake a product evaluation stage or have undertaken a flawed product evaluation process with the resultant contribution to project failure. These latter studies are based on ERP implementation failures that by their very nature are organization wide in terms of impact and change. The decision not to follow a sound evaluation process within these projects led to high levels of user resistance and a plethora of contributory failure factors. In the case of Pan et al. (2008), the organization initiated a formal evaluation and selection process for a company-wide ERP system, but was overruled by the executive who favored a rival product. This decision resulted in a product solution being forced on the stakeholders and contributed to the overall failure of the project.

2.3.6 Inadequate Management Structure and Support

Organizations that fail to establish the required management processes or management structure for project delivery are increasing their chances of failure. The case of the collapsed Australian telecommunications company One.Tel demonstrates the ramifications of a failed project that did not have a formal management and support structure in place. These factors were highlighted as being significant during the period when the company struggled to manage a rapid increase in customers from tens of thousands to 750,000 in a short space of time (Avison and Wilson 2002). Any failings in the management structure are accentuated in the context of remote or split site projects, where the teams are spread across different geographical locations. The offshore development project as outlined by Philip et al. (2009) highlights the critical issues and negative consequences on the project where the organization fails to implement appropriate structures for the management of the project. The study highlighted the ill-defined roles and responsibilities of the onshore/offshore management and team structure and the resulting communication issues, misunderstanding of requirements, and unclear objectives (Philip et al. 2009)

2.3.7 Inadequate Postmortem Process

The inability of organizations and the IS industry as whole to learn from past project failure is a bewildering fact. In a study of 82 US-based organizations, Ewusi-Mensah and Przasnyski (1995) attempted to characterize the postmortem activities undertaken on failed or abandoned projects. The study identified a pattern where organizations seem to repeat past mistakes, highlighting that only 19 % of the organizations carried out a project postmortem review and 60 % of the study group indicated that projects failed for more or less the same reasons as previous projects. The reticence within organizations to conduct postmortem reviews is supported by Verner et al. (2008), highlighting only a small percentage of organizations conducted post-project reviews from a sample of 304 projects. The study identified that those organizations that conducted postmortems were almost entirely for successful projects. The inability to face up to project failure has plagued the IS industry for decades and is unlikely to result in different outcomes unless a step change in willingness to review failed projects is made within organizations. Lessons can be learned from each and every project even if the project is a failure (Kerzner 2013). This needs to be coupled with the removal of a systemic reluctance to share lessons learned with other organizations, and the wider industry as a whole to learn the lessons from failure. In some organizations, the executive and senior management are keen to wind down the resources allocated to projects nearing completion and reallocate them elsewhere, often resulting in the project manager focusing on the new project rather than conducting a lessons learned assessment of the current project. The analysis of the underlying reasons why organizations fail to consistently embrace the postmortem processes on failed IS projects is an area where further research could yield new insights.

2.4   People-Related Failure Factors

The grouping of failure factors in this section is as follows:

- Poor change management and user resistance
- Poor executive support and project sponsorship
- Poor contractor and stakeholder relationship
- Lack of staff commitment, motivation, performance, and turnover issues

2.4.1   Poor Change Management and User Resistance

A large number of studies cite people-related aspects that can be attributed to poor change management and resistance to change as major factors in the failure of IS projects (Barker and Frolick 2003; Beynon-Davies 1995; Fitzgerald and Russo 2005; Hirschheim and Newman 1988; Keil et al. 1998; McGrath 2002; Mitev 1996). Factors relating to aspects of change management have been identified as critical to project outcomes by organizations that have attempted to implement Enterprise Resource Planning (ERP) solutions, highlighting that half of ERP projects end in failure with many citing change management issues as the root cause (Barker and Frolick 2003; Pan et al. 2008; Scott and Vessey 2000). These cases highlight the lack of focus on people-related practices within each of the projects, in particular, lack of user involvement at an early stage, poor communication of changed processes, and lack of change management methodology leading to user resistance issues and ultimate project failure.

Widely cited IS project failures such as the London Ambulance LASCAD project (Beynon-Davies 1995) highlight the significant risks of too high a focus on the project management deliverables while ignoring many of the change management aspects of a project that can prepare the ground for user adoption and help to mitigate the potential for high levels of user resistance. The LASCAD project was an attempt by the London Ambulance Service to automate the tracking and directing of ambulances and their crew to respond to 999 calls to eliminate many of the incumbent manual process. However, during the first day of live operations ambulance crews grew frustrated at the levels of incorrect allocations to incidents; additionally staff at the control center were unable to deal with the high level of exception messages and status updates. These issues led to the system effectively collapsing on the first day of live operations with ambulance call-out times of up to 3 h and ultimately resulting in loss of patient life as a direct result of the failure (Beynon-Davies 1995; Fitzgerald and Russo 2005; McGrath 2002). Other studies that focus on the health sector (Brown and Jones 1998; Gauld 2007) highlight the failure of the organization in preparing the staff for change and the inability of the project executive to convince stakeholders of the direction of change. The cultural aspects of change in large organizations such as the NHS highlight a fragmented structure of subcultures, each of which needs to be the subject of separate stakeholder analysis (Pettigrew et al. 1992). The failed SNCF Socrate project highlights the lack of user engagement and aspects of poor people management as key factors. The Socrate project went live in 1993 and was labeled as a disaster with long queues of angry passengers, failed reservation systems, trains running with no passengers, and railway unions calling their staff out on strike as a direct consequence of the failed system (Mitev 1996). Other large public sector project failures such as those outlined in Warne and Hart (1997) and Winklhofer (2001) highlight the impact of organizational conflicts and some of the negative aspects of organizational change. The large public sector integration project as outlined in Warne and Hart (1997) highlights the significant impact of cultural and political aspects of change in organizations. In this particular case, although modern project management techniques were used, the project had full executive support, and extensive user involvement was provided for, issues relating to change management were still a major factor in the failure of the project (Warne and Hart 1997). The complexities of user resistance and the omission by project managers to fully understand the social and political nature of organizational change can be key factors in the success or failure of IS projects (Hirschheim and Newman 1988). These issues potentially highlight a gap in the practitioner skillset or the inability of organizations to invest in change management.

Although limited by their participation group, studies that predominantly survey the experiences of project managers (Attarzadeh and Ow 2008; Keil et al. 1998; Lemon et al. 2002; Schmidt et al. 2001; Standing et al. 2006; Yeo 2002) highlight the issues faced by IS professionals in relation to change management and support the premise that failing to incorporate the user involvement and user commitment aspects of change management (thereby taking steps to mitigate user resistance issues) are key failure factors. As far back as the 1970s, researchers have highlighted the issues surrounding user resistance (Lucas 1975) and the implications for projects failing to understand and manage the needs of stakeholders. Historically, very few organizations identified, planned, and managed user adoption with many projects instigating change management as part of delivery (Ward and Elvin 1999). More recent studies (e.g. Bartis and Mitev 2008; Klaus and Blanton 2010) highlight the failings of organizations that do not explicitly incorporate processes to manage user resistance and, therefore, fail to reap the benefits of undertaking change management practices early in the project lifecycle. Generally, the literature that cites lack of user involvement, user resistance, or change management aspects (Beynon-Davies 1995; Brown and Jones 1998; Bussen and Myers 1997; Fitzgerald and Russo 2005; Gauld 2007; Hirschheim and Newman 1988; Keil et al. 1998; Lemon et al. 2002; McGrath 2002; Mitev 1996), as causes of project failure, omits to quantify the change management maturity of an organization or whether any formal methodology or guidance such as Prosci® or CMBoK was used within the project. This suggests an oversight in the research with studies failing to ascertain if the change management-related problems were due to organization failings, methodology issues, or leadership and cultural problems.

Studies have shown that aspects of poor change management are a major factor in the failure of IS projects, but by actively engaging with stakeholders during project initiation ensuring users clearly understand the project goals, objectives, benefits, and risks, organizations can help to mitigate user resistance issues further on in the project lifecycle (Project Management Institute 2014). The leadership team must formulate a strategy that engenders a culture within the organization to develop a stakeholder base that is receptive to change. This entails communicating the need for the change, constructing the capability to physically make the change, and setting out the change agenda. Managing the necessary change to organizations appears to be getting more rather than less difficult, and more rather than less important, requiring organizations to develop a core competence to be able to manage change successfully (Burnes 2005). Leading change involves action by people at every level of the business (Pettigrew and Whipp 1993), and the process of sustaining this change is dependent on the interplay of multiple factors on different levels of analysis and time frames (Buchanan et al. 2005). These key factors are incorporated within modern change management methodologies and guidance such as those outlined in Prosci (2012) and Change Management Institute (2013). Incorporating these best practices and the closer integrating of change management processes and methods with project management methodologies is one of the key challenges to the consistent delivery of successful IS projects.

2.4.2 Poor Executive Support and Project Sponsorship

Nixon et al. (2012) and Young (2005) argued that in the context of project outcomes, leadership and top management support are crucial to the success or failure of a project. In all of the five annual benchmarking reports carried out by Prosci®, spanning 10 years and 1400 participant organizations, the role of the executive sponsor was identified as the number one contributor to project success. Furthermore, the benchmark study identified the effectiveness of the sponsor as one of the strongest predictors of project success or failure (Prosci 2012). Executive management support is listed as the top factor for success in the 2013 CHAOS report. The report highlighted the key role of commitment to the project and engendering a consensus among stakeholders, linking this to the vision of the project (Standish Group 2013). Studies of IT professionals (Emam and Koru 2008; Keil et al. 1998; Lemon et al. 2002; Schmidt et al. 2001; Standing et al. 2006) detail the many examples where practitioners have emphasized the major risks to projects from poor executive sponsorship. These studies have highlighted the instances where the executive lacked the commitment to the project, was ineffective, or offered poor leadership and support. The participants in the study carried out by Keil et al. (1998) stated that the number one risk to the project was a lack of top management commitment. The abandoned Executive Information System (EIS) implementation at New Zealand manufacturing company—Gardenco—highlights the major issues faced by projects stemming from the lack of an executive sponsor and a general absence of tangible support from the board (Bussen and Myers 1997). The ERP implementation failure as outlined by Pan et al. (2008) emphasizes the impact of inadequate executive leadership and management structure. In this project, the executive overruled the evaluation committees' selection of an ERP solution and appointed the finance director as the project manager (Pan et al. 2008). The Health Information System (HIS) project failure as detailed by Gauld (2007) highlighted that the sponsoring group failed to convince the clinical staff of the choice of system leading to significant resistance from key stakeholders. The appointment of a suitable project sponsor is a key fundamental decision at the commencement of a project. A sponsor who is inexperienced, too low in the organizational structure to have influence, and too busy to devote enough time to the project or does not have the required personal traits to drive the project forward is unlikely to contribute to a successful outcome. If the organization has a track record of poor project delivery, the reality may be that executives may not wish to be associated with any new initiative and will, therefore, delegate sponsorship to a lower level manager, thereby limiting the project's chances of success at the onset.

2.4.3 Poor Contractor and Stakeholder Relationship

The relationship between an organization that has either outsourced a project to a contracting entity or has employed an external consultant to deliver significant portions of a project can be problematic if not managed effectively. Inevitably, due to the size and complexity of some IS projects, there will be a significant legal contract between the organizations that is meant to govern the relationship between the parties and identify the responsibilities for delivery, quality, and so on. All too often it is the ability of the contract to be interpreted in different ways that results in expensive legal battles when projects fail as each party seeks to apportion blame and gain redress. Studies highlight that postmortems on large project failures that involve a contractor or consultant relationship often state that either the consultant was shown to not have the skills to complete the project (Nawi et al. 2011; Verner and Abdullah 2012) or the consultant underestimated the project scope and complexity (Yeo 2002). Additionally, the interrelationship between organizational power and politics and the conflicts between users and developers as outlined by Warne and Hart (1997), highlighting the complexities of large outsourced projects. These issues perhaps mask a plethora of underlying reasons that signify a fundamental breakdown in the organization and supplier relationship. The case outlined in Brown and Jones (1998) emphasizes a specific case of failure where the organization was shown to have not prepared for change and was inexperienced in working with contractors. These factors coupled with problems managing the contractor relationship and issues with the users being intimidated by, and not fully understanding the methods employed by the contractor to facilitate requirements and gain acceptance of key design aspects, greatly contributed to the failure of the project (Brown and Jones 1998). The failed ERP implementation at Singapore-based Maxima Inc. as outlined in Pan et al. (2008) highlights the major impact of disputes between the organization and contractor, demonstrating the inability of executives to fully assess costs and the subsequent impact on the project benefits and viability.

2.4.4 Lack of Staff Commitment, Performance, Motivation, and Turnover Issues

Projects should focus on those aspects of staff involvement that affect both employee motivation and organizational outcomes to get the best from the project team as a whole (Michie and West 2004). Large projects can be subject to lengthy timescales of many months and sometimes years with the project team likely to suffer from staff turnover and organizational changes to the leadership team and project sponsor. All of these changes have the potential to affect the motivation and performance of the project team (Newman and Sabherwal 1996; Rob 2003). Bussen and Myers (1997) highlighted the issues associated with elongated timescales and its effect on staff commitment and enthusiasm for the project. Conway and Limayem (2011) identified a reduction in performance, increased cynicism, and stress levels due to temporal dissonance among distributed teams of IT workers. The culture within IS-based organizations has for decades been one of staff expected to complete the task at hand. All too frequently software development staff are not rewarded for long hours as projects struggle to deliver to unrealistic timescales (Verner et al. 2008). The failed software projects viewed from the developer perspective outlined by Linberg (1999) highlight that job satisfaction does not have a direct association with the meeting of timescales and identified the disparity of views between developers and IS management. The study raised the issues of excessive workload, individual and team temperament among developers, and its potential to impact project outcomes both positively and negatively. In the context of the value of team-based working leading to successful project outcomes, best results will be gained from organizations developing a team-based culture in which education and communication systems, people management, and reward systems are all geared toward managing teams rather than individuals (Michie and West 2004).

2.5 A Proposed Framework for Understanding IS Failure

Sauer (1993) reviewed the concepts of failure as outlined in Lyytinen and Hirschheim (1987), in particular some of the limitations of *expectation failure*. The study highlighted the inevitability of some level of dissatisfaction among stakeholders, and that the concept of *expectation failure* fails to discriminate between different types of problem situations affecting stakeholders. Sauer (1993) developed an alternative account and model of failure and characterized the relationship between information system components as a *triangle of dependences*. The model presented by Sauer depicts an information system that functions through its reliance on the project organizations' activities and support from stakeholders that require some form of reimbursement from the system. The model consisted of three components: *system*, *supporters*, and *project organization*. Sauer (1993) hypothesized that if unresolved problems are present in any one of the three components of the model, the consequence could be withdrawal of support for the system and ultimately result in system failure. Support for the system can change depending on how stakeholders perceive the system in the context of their own self-interests, potential benefits, and the result of external pressures to continue support for the system. *The triangle of dependencies* has been referenced in a number of studies (Dwivedi et al. 2013a, b; Pan et al. 2008; Yeo 2002), but the literature has failed to develop the model in the light of new understandings of stakeholder behaviors and practices.

We propose the *"The Actuality Failure* (AF)" framework (illustrated in Fig. 2.1) that extends the Sauer (1993) *triangle of dependencies* to represent the concept of the system, the change, and the key aspects of stakeholder support post-project delivery. The separation of the *change* and *system* components in the AF framework reflects the fact that the project not only delivers an IS but also delivers associated changes to processes and working practices. The importance of stakeholder support for these key areas has been referenced in previous IS project failures studies (Barker and Frolick 2003; Beynon-Davies 1995; Fitzgerald and Russo 2005; Hirschheim and Newman 1988; Keil et al. 1998; McGrath 2002; Mitev 1996), highlighting the criticality of these aspects.

The AF framework is characterized as two time-bound segments: *project implementation* and *post-implementation*. This represents the evolving structure of the project and change organization after delivery of the system and the subsequent change in the bounds of support. These aspects are not explicit within the model presented in Sauer (1993). The components of the model are:

- *Change*—the changes to the users working practices and processes as a result of the IS project and implementation.

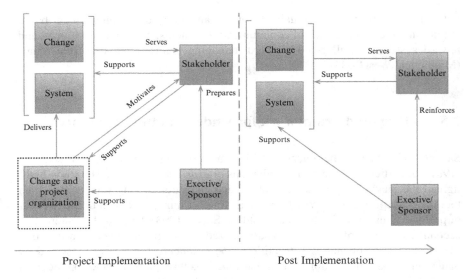

Fig. 2.1 Proposed actuality failure framework (*Source*: Extended from Sauer 1993)

- *System*—the information system developed by the project that is intended to deliver specific benefits to the stakeholders and organization.
- *Change and project organization*—the temporary structure that is established to develop and deliver the project and associated changes to the organization.
- *Stakeholder*—the users and supporters of the system.
- *Executive/Sponsor*—the nominated senior manager from the organization that is tasked with owning the vision of the project and driving the project forward.

During *project implementation* support is provided to the change and project organization from the executive and stakeholders in the context of delivering the system and associated changes. Failure can result if support for the project organization, system, or change is withdrawn from either the stakeholder or executive.

During the *post-implementation* period the system and subsequent changes to working processes and procedures have been delivered, but the project organization structure has been disbanded or scaled down ready for handover to the business. Support for the system can be withdrawn during this period unless effort is made by the executive to ensure the changes are embedded within the organization. This requires sustained reinforcement actions to maintain momentum and adoption of the new system and associated changes. These activities are vital to assure user engagement and support for the realization of the project benefits. These topics are covered in more detail in Sects. 2.4 and 2.5.

The proposed AF framework is based on a review of the existing literature and the identification of potential shortfalls within existing models of failure. It is recognized that the AF framework is as yet a theoretical proposition requiring academic empirical validation.

2.6   Discussion and Concluding Points on Project Failure

Key Points for Practitioners

- Poor project sponsorship is likely to lead to a failed project—take steps to ensure the role is performed effectively.
- Large projects have little chance of being delivered successfully.
- Omitting to take account of the *people* aspects of projects will limit the chances of project success.
- Periodic audit can highlight key factors at an early stage, embrace the process, and encourage review.
- Projects must be continually measured against their business case to ensure benefits are still relevant and can be realized.
- Develop a project culture that encourages people to speak up and raise issues either formally or informally to ensure problems are addressed.

The inability to manage change within organizations and the resulting user resistance and reinforcement issues encountered within projects are frequently cited by studies as reasons for project failure. Previous studies (Hirschheim and Newman 1988; Ward and Elvin 1999) have highlighted the technical bias of project management and the fact that few organizations have planned, actively managed, and sustained business change. Modern formal project management methodologies have progressed from the historical measures of exclusive reliance on time, cost, and quality, to include some change management aspects, but it is questionable whether this is of adequate quality and detail to be sufficient for the practicing project manager. The PRINCE2® guidance set out in OGC Group (2013) defines a product titled: *communications management strategy* that describes the means and frequency of communications with stakeholders. However, this caters for the method of stakeholder communication only, failing to address many of the fundamental people-related issues of resistance or adoption. Terminology between standards is also an issue; references to change management in the PRINCE2® guidance refer to configuration control of changes to scope in the context of product delivery not the people aspects of change. The PMBoK® guide as set out in Project Management Institute (2014) contains a section titled *Project Stakeholder Management* that details how to identify, plan, manage, and control stakeholder engagement on the project but does not provide any formal methods on how to drive change. The guidance set out in both of these widely used de facto texts seems inadequate on both the strategic and detailed elements of managing change and mitigating user resistance. Neither standard refers to an appropriate change management approach or methodology. Professional project management practitioners are aware of change management and will understand the importance of aligning the project and change initiative to keep both activities in step in terms of tasks and deliverables. However, the planning and synchronization of these two areas is largely omitted from the PRINCE2® and PMBoK® guidance. With studies highlighting that 48 % of projects suffer from ineffective stakeholder management (Nelson 2007), this seems to be a stark omission from the project management standards. The net effect of this is that organizations are in danger of implementing change management *light* on their projects. Project managers may adhere to the guidance outlined in the selected project management methodology but then fail to incorporate the required people-related processes to the necessary depth and rigor. This may result in user resistance problems and stakeholder dissatisfaction. The analysis and potential benefits of project and change management processes in the context of an integrated methodology should be the subject of further academic research.

Many organizations attempt to identify failure early on in the project lifecycle by undertaking periodic reviews and stage audits. UK Government public sector projects of a specific size are subject to gateway reviews where the project is audited before commencing to the next stage. Private sector organizations are not subject to the same rules regarding end of stage audit and can choose to enforce periodic audit or initiate a more informal method to assure assessment of progress. Previous studies of project failure have referenced inaccurate status reporting and suboptimal quality control (Jones 2006; Verner et al. 2008) as contributory failure factors but have largely omitted citing the lack of audit or a poor audit function within the organization. Studies have attempted to highlight potential failure by defining early warning signs (Kappelman et al. 2006) that can be monitored by the organization. However, the concept is limited by its simplicity; a missing business case is an early warning sign, but a weak business case or poor set of requirements may not be as easily identifiable at an early stage in the lifecycle. Organizational or operational issues have often been brought into the public domain via whistle-blowers who have exposed serious problems within the organization. However, engendering a culture within an organization or project that encourages whistle-blowing (Park et al. 2009) relies on the willingness of the individual to report bad news and their perception of the potential impact framed in terms of harm to others on the project team. Organizations that are able to create a culture where an agreed whistle-blowing model is the norm could identify potential failure factors early enough to avoid project failure. This needs further academic research to fully identifying the potential benefits and drawbacks.

The subject of project management and methodological performance has largely been omitted from studies of IS project failure. Some studies (Avison and Wilson 2002; Beynon-Davies 1995) have highlighted that either no formal methodology was applied or one was used but not applied correctly. Large IS failures such as those referenced in Gauld (2007), Mitev (1996), Pan et al. (2008), and Verner and Abdullah (2012) implicitly reference the characteristics of a project management methodology and structure but do not provide the detail of any named methodology. References to agile methods can be found in Standish Group (2013) but only in the context of running small projects to potentially deliver in shorter timescales. The recommendations of a number of studies (Dwivedi et al. 2013b; Gibson 2004; Heeks 2006; Keider 1974; Nelson 2007; Nixon et al. 2012) implicitly reference aspects or elements of project management methodology, i.e., risk management, requirements management, user resistance, but make little reference to a formal methodological approach to project management. Studies such as Warne and Hart (1997) highlight that project failure occurred even though modern project management techniques were used. However, it is unclear from the study if there were limitations on their suitability or application that contributed to failure. Poor project management is a factor listed in a number of IS failure studies, but it is not stated whether these failings are methodology based in terms of how the methodology was applied or if the failings were a direct result of the project manager not undertaking his or her duties. The literature seems to have largely omitted to focus much attention on the actual work and performance of the project manager in terms of management style, role, and function (Söderlund 2004), but these aspects could have a huge bearing on project outcomes both positive and negative. The inability or omission of academic studies to tackle the issues of project management methodologies and performance is at best a gap in the research or at least an indicator that these factors have not been explicitly considered in the analysis of failure in IS projects.

The problems encountered in delivering large and complex projects has been cited in a number of studies (Gauld 2007; Jones 2004, 2006; Mitev 1996; Nawi et al. 2011; Verner and Abdullah 2012), but organizations continue to create large IS projects with negligible change in approach or methodology. As recently as 2013, industry-wide studies (Standish Group 2013) have highlighted that small projects have a greater than 70 % chance of performing well, whereas a large project has virtually no chance of coming in on time, on budget, or within scope. The problems with large projects at face value seem obvious: it appears unrealistic to expect users to define up-front and in detail their requirements for a large and complex system. Requirements are likely to change over time, especially for long lead projects. Large projects can have huge change implications on the organization due to the complexity and impact of the project. Additionally, the potential involvement of large numbers of external consultants and technicians within an organization that needs to adapt to a change in culture for the duration of the project can create many problems. Studies that have reviewed the pattern of large project failure (Cable 2009; Standish Group 2013) have proposed a number of recommendations: (a) break up the project into smaller more manageable subprojects each running as an autonomous project in its own right, (b) reduce scope and create smaller projects, and (c) run project along agile lines to deliver incrementally and to shorter timescales. These suggestions may have the potential to yield different outcomes but rely on the organization to recognize a large project and take the steps necessary to change its processes accordingly.

A number of studies have presented frameworks and models to identify and help avoid project failure (Bronte-Stuart 2009; Cule et al. 2000; Goulielmos 2005; Heeks 2006; Lyytinen and Hirschheim 1987; Sauer 1993). Further studies (Young 2005) have challenged this approach citing the lack of relevance of academic research and question whether the research effort to date has been misdirected as it has had little impact on successful outcomes. Scott and Vessey (2000) suggested that due to the scale and complexity of projects, failure at some level is inevitable. Sitkin (1992) hypothesized whether failure is really a negative concept and proposed a theory for organization learning and hypothesized that firms that focus on success suffer the consequent liabilities of success. Sitkin (1992) proposed an alternative approach to failure and suggested that organizations should embrace small failures as an intrinsic component of the learning process and not conceal or avoid failure. The merits of this approach have yet to be fully explored within the IS research community, but Agile-based project management approaches have implicitly incorporated the concept of failure as part of the iterative development process. Projects run along agile lines do not attempt to get the deliverables right first time but rely upon user feedback to make changes to each iteration or sprint as the project evolves.

We have proposed an extension to the *triangle of dependencies* model as outlined in Sauer (1993) to highlight an alternative view of how a system is supported by the stakeholders during pre- and post-implementation and encourage further academic review and analysis of its application.

This section has exposed a number of areas in the literature that would benefit from further research. The key topics are outlined in the highlighted box below:

Recommendations for Future Research

1. Failure has been a fact of life for IS projects for decades despite a mature set of standards and methods that attempt to avoid it, when failure is perhaps inevitable (Scott and Vessey 2000; Sitkin 1992). Can the expectation of failure be formalized as part of the business as usual process and be managed to assure more successful outcomes?
2. The literature has identified the dismal track record of delivering large projects (Standish Group 2013), but this pattern does not seem to change. Is there a case for the development of a *large project* methodology that caters for the specific complexities of this genre of project?
3. The unrealistic expectations of developing an up-front detailed set of requirements for a large complex system has featured in many instances of IS failure; is there a different approach that can yield better outcomes?
4. Studies have highlighted the large number of projects failing due to poor project management, but the literature has failed to focus much attention on the underlying reasons for these failings (Söderlund 2004). Impacts of management style, role, and function could be significant to project outcomes, yet this area is an under researched topic.
5. The lack of academic focus on the suitability, benefits, and limitations of specific project management standards and methodologies is a core area in need of further research.
6. The role of the whistle-blower has been a key feature in exposing some of the problems and practices inherent in large organizations. Could engendering a culture of openness and willingness to highlight problems in large projects result in critical issues being raised and dealt with thereby helping to mitigate failure?
7. The presented AF framework is a theoretical proposition that is yet to be empirically tested. Further research is recommended to validate the framework.

This section has presented the principles and components of project failure highlighting the many root causes and associated complexities in delivering IS projects. A framework has been proposed that models a systems relationship with its stakeholders, the project and the executive. The section highlights that fact that projects fail for a variety of reasons; there is no single root cause, but there are common factors that are highlighted in studies where the same mistakes seem to be repeated within the industry and often in the same organization. Tackling these root causes is a key challenge both for the academic community and industry as a whole.

Summary of Key Points

- Traditional measurement elements of time, cost, and quality do not adequately classify a project as a success or a failure as they omit many of the people-related factors such as adoption and benefits realization.
- Project failure is rarely due to one single factor but the result of a combination of factors.
- Organizations have a tendency to repeat past mistakes failing to learn the lessons of poor project delivery.
- Projects fail despite the use of modern project management standards and methodologies.
- Large project failure has been so catastrophic for the organizations concerned that the project failure has resulted in the collapse of the organization itself.
- Large projects have an increased level of failure over smaller projects with a virtual zero chance of success.
- Failure at some level is inevitable, especially on large projects.

Chapter 3 details the problems defining project success from alternative stakeholder perspectives and sets out the principles of project success in the context of the key critical factors that studies have associated with successful project delivery.

Chapter 3
An Analysis of the Components of Project Success

In the previous section, we dealt with the complexities in defining project failure and the underlying factors that cause projects to fail. In order to deliver projects that have consistent successful outcomes we need to understand project success itself, what success looks like, how it is defined, and the characteristics of projects that are delivered successfully. These topics are discussed in this section.

The narrative starts with characterizing how success is defined within organizations and the problems that can arise in the interpretation of success by different stakeholders. The section then goes on to explain the development of critical success factors (CSFs) and how these can be used to help assure successful project outcomes. The remaining subsections explain some of the key areas on project management success, project performance, and the influences of methodological approaches on success.

3.1 Characterization of Project Success

The body of literature takes a multidimensional approach to project success and its constituents but is not always consistent in its use of terms relating to success. Project success factors or CSFs are the set of conditions, events, and circumstances that can be used by the project organization to increase the chances of successful project outcomes. Project success criteria are the list of principles and standards used to determine or judge project success (Ika 2009). Project success criteria (also termed acceptance criteria in some studies) should be formally agreed with the key stakeholders during the early stages of the project to avoid any acceptance issues during implementation. The practitioner guidance uses the terms product and project acceptance criteria to describe success criteria at the deliverable and overall project levels (OGC Group 2013; Project Management Institute 2014).

© The Author(s) 2016   27
D.L. Hughes et al., *Success and Failure of IS/IT Projects*,
SpringerBriefs in Information Systems, DOI 10.1007/978-3-319-23000-9_3

The principles and constituents of IS project success, at face value, do not seem complex or multifaceted, put simply—*ensure the customer is happy and the project is delivered on time and budget to the agreed set of requirements*. But when project-based success is scrutinized further, questions arise: who defines success? How is it judged and by what criteria? Is success defined at a project level or on the basis of overall stakeholder satisfaction? Is success viewed differently depending on the stakeholder type? A project can be a success for one party and a disaster for another (de Wit 1988). These issues have challenged many researchers, leading some to conclude that project management cannot deliver absolute success, but only the perception of success and that the evaluation of success may change over time (Baker et al. 1983). Researchers have questioned the concepts of success criteria and conclude that success is more complex and multidimensional than traditional measures and that no consensus exists among the academic community as to what constitutes project success (Atkinson 1999; Morris and Hough 1987; Müller and Judgev 2012; Pinto and Slevin 1988).

Project success can be attributed as having hard and soft dimensions; the hard dimensions of a project are tangible, objective, and relatively easy to measure. The soft dimensions that refer to stakeholder happiness, job satisfaction, and enhanced reputation are much more problematic to measure as they are subtle and subjective (Baccarini 1999). Traditionally, project success has been measured in terms of specific technical factors, namely, time, cost, and quality—often termed the iron triangle. However, although providing a benchmark of delivery, many researchers have concluded that these factors do not provide a firm basis to define whether a project is a success or a failure, as they measure the technical elements only (Atkinson 1999; Baker et al. 1983; de Wit 1988; Jugdev and Müller 2005; Kenny 2003; Sauer 1993; Shenhar et al. 2001). Researchers have attempted to extend the traditional technical measures to provide a more balanced view of success that includes additional success criteria. Atkinson (1999) criticized how project success was measured and proposed an extension to the iron triangle—the *square root*, as a new mechanism to measure success criteria. The model included information system aspects and organizational and stakeholder benefits to attempt to provide a more balanced and realistic indication of success. Wateridge (1998) criticized the traditional measures of success and argued that measuring time, cost, and specification takes a very narrow view of success criteria. The study proposed a set of *criteria for success* that were empirically tested against project manager, sponsor, and user participants. The findings highlighted the short-term technical oriented criteria, used by project managers (often set by senior management), which were used in preference to stakeholder satisfaction-based criteria. Wateridge recommended that projects define project success criteria as an early stage activity to mitigate any bias later on in the project (Wateridge 1998).

The measurement of project success is also viewed differently not only by stakeholder type but also from the perspective of internal project role. Developers tend to link the success of a completed project to the quality of the product and job satisfaction in being involved with creativity and learning on the project (Linberg 1999; Procaccino et al. 2005), whereas project managers tend to balance the needs of stakeholder satisfaction and organizational benefits to gauge success (Dwivedi et al. 2015b). The views of project success can differ greatly from the client and project team perspectives, especially in circumstances where the project team is an external contracting organization. Success from the viewpoint of the contracting organization is likely to be based on whether the project delivered financial benefits to the contractor in the short or medium term, with stakeholder satisfaction potentially demoted further down the list of success measures unless these aspects are formally included within the criteria for success and agreed during project initiation. Although centered on Private Finance Initiative (PFI) themes, Bryde and Robinson (2005) surveyed a cross section of UK-based staff from contractor and client organizations to gain a perspective on the differing emphasis of success criteria. The study highlighted the potential mismatch between stakeholder and project practices of measuring success, highlighting a barrier to effective client–contractor working relationships. This mismatch in perspectives of success from the different parties is an underlying issue that must be clarified at an early stage in the project as part of the acceptance criteria to mitigate risk further on in the project. The importance of agreeing what constitutes project success is critical in fixed price projects where the contractor will effectively deliver to the stated contractual requirements and treat any other dimensions of success as effectively a change to the specification.

There is general agreement within the body of literature that success cannot be measured by a single factor, but requires a set of interrelated and interdependent measures (DeLone and McLean 1992; Rana et al. 2013, 2015a, b). A number of success models and frameworks have been proposed that attempted to provide a formative definition of project success (Bannerman and Thorogood 2011; Howsawi and Eager 2014). The widely cited DeLone and McLean IS Success Model identified six components of IS success: *system quality*, *information quality*, *use*, *user satisfaction*, *individual impact*, and *organizational impact* (DeLone and McLean 1992). The research articulated the issues inherent in measuring success and highlighted the problems within organizations where success is measured based on the user participation element being the primary measure. The user participation approach fails to include the system and information quality aspects and the fact that user assessment of success can be highly variable (DeLone and McLean 1992). DeLone and McLean reviewed the proposed extensions to their original model 10 years after its original publication and revised the model to include *service quality* and *net benefits* in place of *organizational* and *individual impacts* in the context of retaining relevance and simplicity in measuring IS success (DeLone and McLean 2003).

The practitioner perspective on the definition of project success is largely based on the guidance within PRINCE2® and PMBoK®. The PMBoK® is surprisingly weak on this subject. The guidance includes a small section that effectively advises that the project should be measured in terms of completing the project within the constraints of scope, time, cost, quality, and risk as approved between project and senior management. The PMBoK® also includes a defined objective for the project manager to modify the organizational behavior to accept the project outcomes (Project Management Institute 2014), failing to clarify if the project outcomes are successful or otherwise. Under its Quality Management Strategy, PRINCE2® makes an implied reference to project success in its advice that a key success factor of any project is that it delivers what the user expects and finds acceptable. The guidance further advises that success definition is stated and agreed at the beginning of a project (OGC Group 2013). This stance is supported in Wateridge (1995), where the study advocates that the criteria for project success be agreed by all parties at the start of the project and constantly reviewed as the project progresses.

3.2   Project Critical Success Factors

In analyzing the constituents of project success, many studies have developed a set of CSFs that are positioned as an essential component in the project managers' toolkit to assure successful project outcomes. The widely cited CSFs as outlined in Pinto and Slevin (1987) are based on the feedback from US-located, part-time MBA students tasked with interpreting success based on their own project experiences. The study identified ten factors: *project mission, top management support, project schedule/plan, client consultation, personnel issues, technical tasks, client acceptance, monitoring and feedback, communication, and troubleshooting* (Pinto and Slevin 1987). The identified factors were developed into a framework that explicitly set out each in a sequenced order with *communication* linked to all of the factors and *troubleshooting* available throughout the entire implementation process. Although the model suggested some interrelationships between the factors, it does not measure the strength of their relationship with success (Pinto and Slevin 1987). The factors were further examined in subsequent empirical studies—Pinto and Slevin (1988) and Pinto and Prescott (1988)—to consider project success from its strategic and tactical perspectives and by extending the factors based on a consideration of the effects at key stages of the project lifecycle. Morris and Hough (1987) developed a set of success factors in the context of an extensive framework depicting the subjective and objective elements of project success, highlighting that success varies across the project and product lifecycle involving a range of stakeholders. Kerzner (1987) related CSFs to the environment, senior management, and projects describing the criticality of interfaces between the internal and external environment, and the importance of project management from the perspective of corporate understanding and executive commitment. Subsequent studies such as Belassi and Tukel (1996) identified the effects that success factors have on project performance and developed a success framework that highlighted the importance of understanding the interrelationships between the factors. More recent studies seem to acknowledge an increased emphasis on the importance of stakeholder involvement, benefits management and project portfolio aspects (Atkinson 1999; Dwivedi et al. 2015b; Fortune and White 2006; Hyvari 2006; Müller and Judgev 2012; Turner 2009), and the role of the sponsor (Jugdev and Müller 2005; Patton and Shechet 2007) as key constituents of CSFs. The widely cited *real* success factors on projects as outlined in Cooke-Davies (2002) attempted to address three fundamental questions: (1) *what factors lead to project management success?* (2) *What factors lead to a successful project?* (3) *What factors lead to consistently successful projects?* The *real* success factors are based on the analysis of 136 mainly European projects from 23 separate organizations with budgets up to $300 million and 10 years duration, with an average project size of $16 million and project duration of two years. The *real* success factors as outlined in Cooke-Davies (2002) are:

- Adequacy of company-wide education on the concepts of risk management.
- Maturity of an organization's process for assigning ownership of risks.
- Adequacy with which a visible risk register is maintained.
- Adequacy of an up-to-date risk management plan.
- Adequacy of documentation of organizational responsibilities on the project.
- Keep project (or project stage duration) below 3 years (1 year is better).
- Allow changes to scope only through a mature scope change control process.
- Maintain the integrity of the performance measurement baseline.
- The existence of an effective benefits delivery and management process.
- Adequate portfolio and program management practices.
- Suite of project, portfolio, and program metrics that provide adequate feedback on project performance.
- An effective means of learning from experience on projects leading to continuous improvement of project management practices.

Cooke-Davies (2002) highlighted that the list of *real* CSFs does not contain any factors that can be explicitly associated with *people factors* and hypothesized that this omission was due to a focus on what people and teams do rather than the quality of the interaction. Additionally, the study asserted that each of the 12 factors implicitly involved people aspects, and as such the *people factors* and its associations with success are integral to each of the factors. The study's CSFs are evidence based from the empirical data; therefore, the omission of people-related factors is a reflection of the processes followed within each of the organizations within the study. However, the soft side of project management, in particular: key aspects of change management, has been shown to be a fundamental area that can greatly contribute to project's success (Hyvari 2006; Müller and Judgev 2012; Turner 2009).

Many strands of project success research have reviewed factors in the context of specific areas of success rather than a comprehensive list of factors to suit all scenarios. These include areas such as requirements (Aslam and Asghar 2008; Alexander 1998), risk management (De Bakker et al. 2010), scope management (Dekkers and Forselius 2007), organizational aspects (Fisk et al. 2010; Gray 2001), and top management performance and support (Kearns 2007; Nixon et al. 2012; Patton and Shechet 2007). The success factors relating to specific genres of projects have also been analyzed in the literature. One of the most prevalent is the research focus on ERP projects where the implementations are complex, spanning many business units, and often require an organization to reengineer its core processes to make best use of the software (Holland et al. 1999). Although the ERP-specific studies reference many of the CSFs identified in previous studies (Jugdev and Müller 2005; Kerzner 1987; Pinto and Prescott 1988; Pinto and Slevin 1987), there is an explicit emphasis on business analysis, redesign of business processes, role of product champion, standardization, and effective communications, especially in the context of the management of change (Nah et al. 2001; Sumner 1999; Umble et al. 2003). ERP implementations that span cross-cultural boundaries are faced with additional complexities often due to a cultural perception of key CSFs. Shanks et al. (2000) reviewed the different emphasis given to specific CSFs in a case study of ERP implementations in Asia and Australia and highlighted the Asian organizations' focus on technical issues, cautious approach to risk, and reduced importance of change management. This contrasts with the Australian organizations' approach with less emphasis on technical factors and more focus on project champion and change management CSFs (Shanks et al. 2000). These factors highlight the cultural aspects of organizations and how this can have an impact on the project and change management approach to realizing success.

Although key sections of the literature have attempted to develop a *one-size-fits-all* set of CSFs suitable for any project across many genres, this poses a dilemma for practitioners and researchers alike. The bulk of the literature that has reviewed CSFs cites one of the key Pinto and Slevin papers (Pinto and Slevin 1987, 1988) or Belassi and Tukel (1996) and attempts to extend the recommended factors or develop additional factors with some studies including an empirical element to support the change of emphasis (Cooke-Davies 2002). It is not clear from the literature as to which set of CSFs would be appropriate, as many of the factors vary in content, scope, and relevance (Wateridge 1998). There is also a considerable overlap between many of the published CSF models and lists of factors, adding to the quandary of the project manager in their selection of appropriate CSFs (Fortune and White 2006). The literature is light on the empirical evidence to identify the key set of CSFs that are used on current projects and how CSFs are applied to different genre projects across varying organization sectors. This leaves the project manager exposed to the risk of selecting inappropriate success factors or having to tailor existing CSFs to suit the specific needs of the project.

3.3   Project Success and Its Relationship with Project Management Success

The literature is divided on the applicability of dividing success into its project and project management components with many omitting to recognize any explicit separation between the factors (Belassi and Tukel 1996; DeLone and McLean 1992; Kliem and Ludin 1992; Pinto and Slevin 1988). The underlying premise of researchers differentiating between project success (the successful delivery of the project objectives) and project management success (time, cost, and quality success measures) is based on a theoretical concept that the two can result in very different outcomes. Distinction has been made between the terms, by describing each in the context of *hard* and *soft* dimensions with the *hard* described as the internal efficiency-based measures or technical elements and *soft* being the people-oriented aspects (Shenhar et al. 2001). Researchers have differentiated between project success and project management success by suggesting that good project management effort should not be seen to be a guarantee for a successful project and, equally, that a successful project is not necessarily the result of good project management (de Wit 1988). Furthermore, success factors have been attributed in some studies to be specifically associated with the project, project management, or those factors attributed with delivering consistently successful projects as a means to highlight the different emphasis and drivers behind the factors (Cooke-Davies 2002). Baccarini (1999) subscribed to the separating of the concepts but referenced the term *product success* described as the successful delivery of a project's final products and asserted that, conceptually, the determination of project management success disregards product success. It is reasonable to accept that the failure of project management could eventually lead to the ultimate failure of the project (unless the management failings were addressed in time to save the project) and the overall project could fail despite the implementation of successful project management (Ika 2009). Additionally, in a scenario where there exists a contractor undertaking the supplier role for a separate customer, it could be argued that the supplier project manager will be judged on the technical deliverables, i.e., delivering a profitable project rather than meeting the needs of the stakeholders. However, if the processes are in place within the project to formalize an agreed acceptance criteria with the key defined stakeholders that represent the delivery of the defined benefits, project and project management success should be closely aligned.

The practitioner guidance from PMBoK® and PRINCE2® does not explicitly differentiate between project success and project management success (Project Management Institute 2014; OGC Group 2013) and one assumes an implicit acceptance that the standards assume good, well-executed project management will give the project the best chance of a successful outcome (Project Management Institute 2014). Although the literature has attempted to develop a reasonable argument to differentiate between project and project management success, the existing research has failed to empirically progress the debate with most papers articulating a conceptual acceptance of the two strands of emphasis (Ika 2009; Cooke-Davies 2002). The responsibility of the project manager is to deliver a successful project in adherence to the defined project acceptance criteria as agreed among the stakeholders during project initiation (OGC Group 2013). If the project manager delivers a project that fulfills the technical criteria of time, cost, and quality but omits to satisfy key stakeholder requirements, then it seems reasonable to suggest that he has not delivered a successful project. Nor has he delivered successful project management as he has failed to ensure stakeholder acceptance. Therefore, the attempt by some of the regularly cited literature to separate project from project manager success seems counterintuitive and a somewhat unnecessary separation of principles that is not empirically supported in the literature. Although not referenced in the previous studies, it could be argued that the differentiation in concepts is somewhat historical in context, in that the attributes of project success as set out in Cooke-Davies (2002) and de Wit (1988) are aligned with some of the concepts and principles set out in most change management standards.

3.4   Project Management Performance and Project Success

The role of the project manager in the delivery of successful project outcomes is critical, especially in the current arena of large, complex technological projects that involve significant change and mobilization of large amounts of resources. The literature highlights an immature understanding of the relationship between project manager performance and project success, lacking a more holistic performance assessment framework (Mir and Pinnington 2014). The success model outlined by Pinto and Slevin (1987), although not explicitly referencing the performance of the project manager as a distinct component, lists the attributes of performance within each factor and exposes performance attributes within the *troubleshooting* factor. Success factors relating to project manager performance are an integral part of the Belassi and Tukel's (1996) success framework where the project manager is judged on *ability to delegate authority, ability to trade off, ability to coordinate, perception of his role and responsibilities, competence, and commitment.* Project management performance success factors are referenced in Cooke-Davies (2002) in the context of performance against budget and schedule. These include *risk management, stage management, scope management, and integrity of performance measurement baseline.* Studies have shown that successful project management is influenced by a wide spectrum of variables depending on project type and technological uncertainty, which, if neglected, could impact on successful outcomes (Shenhar et al. 2001). Project managers who are able to demonstrate leadership and sound judgment and possess the capability to deconstruct complex processes into simple understandable tasks have a greater chance of success (Standish Group 2013).

There is a general consensus in the literature that the traditional technical measures of success, namely, time, cost, and quality, are inadequate (Atkinson 1999; Baker et al. 1983; de Wit 1988; Jugdev and Müller 2005; Sauer 1993; Shenhar et al. 2001), leading to the inclusion of stakeholder success criteria in the overall success framework. One of the consequences of increased success criteria is the additional performance measures placed on the project manager in the overall assessment of project success and the complexities inherent in a more subjective set of criteria (Bryde 2008). The performance of the project manager has been analyzed in Bryde (2003), where the study presents the Project Management Performance Assessment (PMPA) model as a framework for identifying characteristics of high performing and low performing project management. The PMPA model contains six elements: *PM leadership, PM staff, PM policy and strategy, PM partnerships and resources, project life cycle management processes, and PM key performance indicators* (Bryde 2003). Subsequent empirical studies (Mir and Pinnington 2014; Qureshi et al. 2009) have reviewed the PMPA model and have identified a positive and significant impact on project management performance and associated probabilities of successful project outcomes.

The study of project actualities in the context of the practitioners' work and performance and the subsequent impact on success has not featured highly in the literature. Studies have historically omitted to focus much attention on the management/

leadership style, role, and function of the project manager (Söderlund 2004; Turner and Müller 2005), but these aspects could have a significant bearing on project outcomes both positively and negatively. This omission in the literature seems surprising given the large number of studies directly identifying project management as a key factor in the failure of projects (Avison and Wilson 2002; Brown and Jones 1998; Emam and Koru 2008; Gauld 2007; Keil et al. 1998; Nawi et al. 2011; Pan et al. 2008; Philip et al. 2009; Standing et al. 2006; Verner and Abdullah 2012; Verner et al. 2008). The Project Management Institute (PMI)-sponsored research undertaken by Turner and Müller (2005) reiterated the gap in the literature in the context of the impact and performance of the project manager. The study highlighted the importance of including the leadership style and competence of the project manager as a success factor. Nixon et al. (2012) and Young (2005) argued that in the context of project outcomes, leadership and top management support are crucial to the success (or failure) of a project. Although limited due to the low response rate (25 participants), the study by Hyvari (2006) of Finland-based project managers highlighted the top critical project manager-related success factors as *commitment, ability to coordinate, and effective leadership*. The study concluded that successful projects are led by project managers demonstrating a combination of technical, managerial, and leadership skills, aligned with the motivation of the project team and strategic aspects of client interaction (Hyvari 2006). Studies have identified that project managers who have delivered successful projects have been shown to exhibit positive leadership behaviors; these attributes can be viewed as being just as important as their project management skills (Sumner et al. 2006).

With the realization that many of the large-scale project failures have been attributed to management failure of some form (Scott and Vessey 2000), the performance of the project manager has been heavily criticized, thus leading to a greater scrutiny of practitioner soft skills and cognitive style to complement the traditional project management capability (Esa and Samad 2014). Project management success is as dependent upon people as it is on the relevant technical and functional skills (Project Management Institute 2014). Creasy and Anantatmula (2013) reviewed the performance aspects of project managers in the context of their personality traits and their association with project outcomes, highlighting the need for greater application of soft skills and their potential impact on project success. Studies that have identified links between soft skills and project success have concluded that these competencies have an equal if not greater contribution to project success than the more standards based, technical and process related hard skills (Lechler and Dvir 2010; Müller and Turner 2007; Sumner et al. 2006).

3.5 Top Management Support and the Role of the Sponsor

Industry-based empirical studies have highlighted the vital role of the sponsor in the success of projects and have identified that an effective and supportive sponsor is the number one contributor to success (Prosci 2012). Based on a survey of

41 project managers, Keil et al. (1998) stated that the number one risk to project success was a lack of top management commitment. Studies of IT professionals (Emam and Koru 2008; Lemon et al. 2002; Schmidt et al. 2001; Standing et al. 2006) highlight the major risks to projects from poor executive sponsorship where the executive was ineffective, lacked commitment to the project, or provided poor leadership and inadequate support. Nixon et al. (2012) and Young (2005) identified that leadership and top management support are critical to the success (or failure) of a project. The role of the project sponsor (or executive) in supporting the project within the organization is explicitly supported within the practitioner literature (OGC Group 2013; Project Management Institute 2014), in which the sponsor and executive are tasked with reinforcing commitment to the project and promoting the benefits the project will deliver. However, although limited studies have identified top management support as a prerequisite for project success (Dwivedi et al. 2015b; Kearns 2007), the role of the project sponsor is an underresearched area with studies relying on lists of sponsor activities and confusing the terms sponsor and champion (Bryde 2008). The literature consistently references positive executive and senior management support as a CSF (Clarke 1999; Davis 2014; Marnewick 2012), but fails to explicitly detail the sponsor contribution and association with project success. Suitable executive sponsors for a project within an organization may be reticent in undertaking the role if they feel they would not be associated with a successful outcome. This may result in middle managers being allocated the role and their low level in the management hierarchy being a potential barrier to key resource allocation, stakeholder buy-in, and budget agreement for the project (Kerzner 2013). The links between sponsor activities and project success were studied in Bryde (2008), where 238 UK-based practitioners were surveyed on their experiences and interactions with sponsors on their projects. The study results highlight that if organizations wish to maximize project success, the project sponsor role must be clearly defined, communicated, and aligned with appropriate training and development (Bryde 2008).

3.6 Methodological Approaches to Success

It seems surprising that the project success literature in the definition of CSFs and their association with project success (Atkinson 1999; Belassi and Tukel 1996; Cooke-Davies 2002; Fortune and White 2006; Morris and Hough 1987; Pinto and Slevin 1987; Pinto and Prescott 1988) omits to make any explicit reference to project management methodology and its contribution to success. One of the more recent and widely cited studies on projects and success factors—Cooke-Davies (2002)—makes reference to portfolio management practices and effective benefits delivery within the 12 *real success factors*, but not in the context of a project management methodology. This theme continues in Bryde (2003) where the presented PMPA model outlines *project life-cycle management processes*, intimating some formality to the structure of managing the business process, but failing to outline any detail of a project methodology. Studies have suggested that the standardization of project practices (Milosevic and Patanakul 2005; Toney and Powers 1997) and excellence in project management (Kerzner 1998) are key project success factors, but fall short in analyzing these aspects in the context of a formal project management methodology and its contribution to success.

With the drive for organizations to train their project managers to practitioner level in one of the major standards, there is an underlying assumption that practitioner professionalization would translate into significant increases in project manager performance leading to successful project outcomes. However, the limited amount of research into this topic has identified only a negligible statistical relationship between performance and adoption of standards (Crawford 2005). Studies have categorized the existing literature as being irrelevant, narrow in focus, or limited due to small sample size (Papke-Shields et al. 2010). Clearly, the literature has not focused on this area and is unable to significantly contribute to the debate on whether project management standards and methodologies can contribute to successful project outcomes. If the statistics on project delivery referenced within industry-based studies such as Standish Group (2013) are accepted as the definitive measure of poor project performance, it is difficult to identify a clear ROI for the many years of increased emphasis on project training, certification, and greater levels of practitioner professionalism.

3.7 Change Management Influence on Project Success

The impacts of omitting the people aspects of project management have been outlined in numerous studies (Barker and Frolick 2003; Beynon-Davies 1995; Fitzgerald and Russo 2005; Hirschheim and Newman 1988; Keil et al. 1998; McGrath 2002; Mitev 1996), highlighting instances where projects did not involve users at an early stage, suffered from poor communication with stakeholders and where projects failed to address the high levels of resistance from users. Project managers must address the social and political nature of organizational change and understand the complexities of user resistance and its impact on the success (or failure) of IS projects (Hirschheim and Newman 1988).

Projects that encourage the early engagement with stakeholders can increase the chances of success by mitigating user resistance issues further on in the project (Project Management Institute 2014). The changes to working practices and business processes as a direct consequence of the project must be strategically managed by the leadership team and sponsor. Sponsor-led initiatives that engender a culture receptive to change can prepare the ground for a successful project. Stakeholders need to be presented with a clear vision of the change to the organization and to be convinced of the need for the change. Success is better served where stakeholders are persuaded by the compelling arguments, rather than a forceful change to their working practices. The overall logic of the changes must be clearly articulated and understood to gain an acceptance momentum among the stakeholder community (Cameron and Green 2012).

In the context of factors that are deemed to be the greatest contributors to change management and, therefore, project success, Prosci (2012) highlighted the following factors from a survey of 650 organizations: *appointment of a project sponsor who is visible and active, ensure open and frequent communication of the proposed change, apply a structured approach to change management, ensure that the project has fully funded dedicated change management resource, take steps to ensure the engagement and participation of stakeholders, ensure that middle management actively supports the changes.* Organizations that have developed high levels of maturity in the application of change management demonstrate an integrated approach to change and project management activities to deliver successful outcomes (Prosci 2012).

3.8 A Proposed Multifactor Success (MfS) Framework

Previous studies have developed extensive lists of CSFs in an attempt to define the key components of successful projects (Belassi and Tukel 1996; Cooke-Davies 2002; Pinto and Prescott 1988; Pinto and Slevin 1987; Tukel and Rom 1998). The CSFs in each of these studies are presented as a set of criteria, which, if followed by the project, could increase the likelihood of success. The literature has also focused on the importance of defining and agreeing success criteria in the context of acceptance of the project (Atkinson 1999; de Wit 1988; Ika 2009). Successful projects are dependent on alignment with an appropriate set of CSFs with the delivery of the project, and associated capability in compliance with an agreed set of success criteria. The literature has attempted to develop various models or frameworks that represent the concepts of success (and failure) (Atkinson 1999; DeLone and McLean 1992, 2003; Fortune and White 2006) but has failed to adequately represent the key fact that an IS project will *almost never* fully satisfy all of the traditional measures of success. The reality is that in the delivery of IS projects, there is always some form of compromise and negotiation in the context of time, cost, quality, timescale of adoption, or the amount and scale of benefits that will be realized. These facts represent the organic nature of projects, highlighting that success is viewed very differently by stakeholder type and requires a set of interrelated and interdependent measures (Bryde and Robinson 2005; DeLone and McLean 1992; Rana et al. 2013, 2015a, b).

The Multifactor Success (MfS) framework illustrated in Fig. 3.1 takes account of the increased emphasis on the stakeholder and benefit realization components of success as highlighted in Cooke-Davies (2002) and DeLone and McLean (2003). The implementation section of the framework represents the project and change management facets of delivery, where success is influenced by the CSFs listed in studies such as Cooke-Davies (2002) and Fortune and White (2006). The separation of the project and change management aspects in the model highlights the different emphasis on these two areas and the implicit association between each section within the CSF literature. Studies have shown that success is significantly influenced by organizations that invest in the planning and effective management of the people

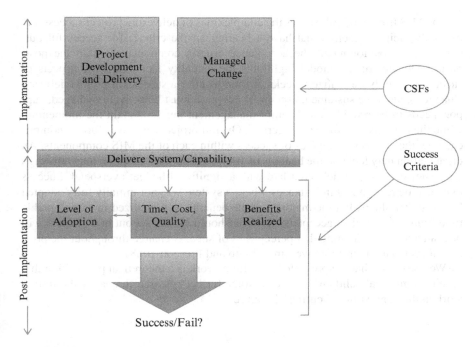

Fig. 3.1 Multifactor success framework

side of projects (Prosci 2012; Standish Group 2013). The post-implementation section of the MfS framework represents a breakdown of each of the main success criteria components that have a significant influence on success:

- *Level of adoption*—acceptance of the system demonstrated by the timescale of actual take-up by users and the adherence to the changed working practices and procedures.
- *Time, cost and quality*—measurement of the technical or project management aspects of success.
- *Benefits realized*—fulfillment of the benefits as outlined in the business case.

Each of these components has a significant influence on outcomes where overall project success or failure can be judged by the inability of the project to fulfill the necessary criteria. The MfS framework illustrates the close links between each of the success criteria components, therefore highlighting the influence that each component can have on the others in the framework. This is best demonstrated by exploring potential project outcomes. For example, a delivered system that has compromised on quality may have a direct impact on the level of user adoption; a system delivered late may not accrue the level of benefits that were envisaged at the start of the project; a system that was delivered over budget requiring cost savings on training and reinforcement activities could have a direct impact on levels of adoption and realization of benefits.

The MfS framework illustrates the complexities of delivering project success and the multiplicity of factors that have a bearing on the criteria for successful outcomes. The positioning of the acceptance criteria components within the post-project element of the model highlights the actuality fact that some aspects of success may only be realized weeks or months after a successful project delivery. Change needs to be sustained, aspects of adoption must be actively managed, support needs to be provided, and senior management must maintain the momentum while the benefits are still being accrued. Overall project success is further complicated by the nuances of degrees of success within each of the MfS components. An organization may feel that the benefits of 100 % stakeholder adoption may outweigh the issues of a project delivered late with a significant budget overspend. Success may also be recognized in instances where a system was not initially fully adopted by the stakeholders, but the majority of the benefits were realized in an acceptable time frame. The project acceptance criteria should clearly set out how success will be realized acknowledging that perceptions of success change throughout the project lifecycle and, therefore, over time (Pinto and Prescott 1988).

We recognize that the presented MfS framework is a theoretical proposition that requires empirical validation. We encourage further research to qualify the framework in the context of the current literature.

3.9 Discussion and Concluding Points on Project Success

The literature has focused significant effort in the identification and measurement of project success but lacks consensus as to what constitutes project success (Atkinson 1999; Morris and Hough 1987; Müller and Judgev 2012; Pinto and Slevin 1988). Studies have presented models and frameworks that have been positioned as tools or instruments in the measurement of project success (Bannerman and Thorogood 2011; DeLone and McLean 1992; Howsawi and Eager 2014). However, project success is a complex and multifaceted concept. Different stakeholders can have diverse perceptions of success (de Wit 1988), and the evaluation of success may change over time (Baker et al. 1983). This presents a dichotomy for the project manager faced with numerous lists of success criteria, each offering a different insight into the key factors that will deliver success. These facts present major challenges to organizations highlighting the critical task of quantifying success criteria early in the project lifecycle to mitigate risks during implementation.

The development of a definitive set of project CSFs has been the subject of a number of studies (Belassi and Tukel 1996; Morris and Hough 1987; Pinto and Slevin 1987), in an attempt to present a set of success factors that can be used by project managers as a mechanism for implementing successful projects. The literature acknowledges the transition from a technical or hard factors perspective to a more inclusive set of CSFs that include benefits delivery and an emphasis on stakeholder satisfaction, leading to increased levels of user adoption (Atkinson 1999; Cooke-Davies 2002; Dwivedi et al. 2015b; Fortune and White 2006;

Hyvari 2006; Müller and Judgev 2012; Turner 2009). The selection of an appropriate set of CSFs is problematic in that the bulk of the literature offers a *one-size-fits-all* set of CSFs that may not be appropriate or even relevant for certain project types. The net effect of this is the risk that project managers may choose an inappropriate set of factors, or having to heavily tailor a perceived *best-fit* set of CSFs that may lead to negative outcomes.

Key Points for Practitioners

- Top management support is a prerequisite for successful projects.
- A framework of CSFs can be used as a guideline or checklist to ensure the bases are covered as the project progresses through its lifecycle.
- Ensuring the project formally defines its acceptance and success criteria as an early stage activity can help to mitigate any ambiguity during delivery.
- Formal project standards and methods provide structure to the management of a project, but success will require the pragmatic application of any guidance to take account of the culture and maturity of the organization.
- Applying change management principles to a project can address resistance and ease the path to adoption.

The literature has attempted to define the key factors for project success based upon empirical studies of projects that were delivered and deemed to be successful from the organization perspective and those based on fulfillment of acceptance criteria and delivery of benefits. Studies have also included the survey of key stakeholders that have been involved in the delivery of successful projects from the project and end user perspectives. However, there are fundamental limitations with this approach. Where a project is deemed to be a success, it is left to the project manager or other stakeholders to set out what they view as the key reasons for that success. The project manager might make the case for the adherence to a formal project management methodology and the end user may highlight the key success factors as the involvement of the stakeholder community at an early stage. Each may be correct, but it is based on their personal perceptions of the reasons for success. The success components as listed in DeLone and McLean (1992) highlight the key areas that organizations can use to measure success. However, pinpointing the key aspects of the project that significantly contributed to its success is based on individual interpretation and personal bias. Weight may be attached to key CSFs where project participant views are surveyed and the data supports the numerical significance of a set of factors over others, for example, the contribution of the dynamic sponsor or the coworking of the project and stakeholder team. However, the views on success are still based on individual perspectives and are by their very nature subjective.

The performance of project managers has been implicitly assessed within a number of studies (Belassi and Tukel 1996; Cooke-Davies 2002; Pinto and Slevin 1987) and explicitly in Bryde (2003) as part of the PMPA model that presents a mechanism for assessing project management performance within projects. Although studies such as Hyvari (2006) have identified the multi-skillset requirements of project managers who deliver successful projects, the literature has largely omitted to focus on the actual work, performance, and leadership style of the project manager (Söderlund 2004; Turner and Müller 2005), ignoring the potential impact on project outcomes (Nixon et al. 2012; Young 2005). The personality traits of successful project managers have been analyzed in some studies (Creasy and Anantatmula 2013), highlighting the need for greater application of soft skills. This stance is supported by the literature with some studies concluding that these competencies have an equal if not greater contribution to project success than traditional skillsets (Lechler and Dvir 2010; Müller and Turner 2007; Sumner et al. 2006).

The literature reinforces the view that one of the key factors for successful projects is the support of top management and an effective and engaged project sponsor (Clarke 1999; Davis 2014; Keil et al. 1998; Marnewick 2012; Prosci 2012; Standish Group 2013). However, although some studies have explored the interactions with project sponsors (Bryde 2008), the academic literature has not focused much attention on the sponsor contribution in any detail to provide insight into the main attributes of the role linked with project success.

Organizations that embrace a formal project management methodology do so, with the expectation that this will increase the chances of project success. However, if the adoption of standards yields only negligible results (Crawford 2005), organizations must question their commitment and investment in formal methods.

This section has exposed a number of areas in the literature that would benefit from further research. The key topics are outlined in the highlighted box below:

Recommendations for Future Research

1. Studies have identified the issues defining success on projects (Atkinson 1999; Morris and Hough 1987; Müller and Judgev 2012; Pinto and Slevin 1988), but there is little research that has identified the issues this presents on the ground to organizations in actuality. Do organizations reach a consensus or pragmatic view on associating success on projects? Is this an academic argument in that organizations are predominantly focused on the delivery of benefits in adherence to agreed acceptance criteria?

2. The literature has focused on the identification of CSFs that are presented as a set of key guidelines to better assure project success. But what are the tangible reasons for success on projects? Is it methodology or the soft skills of the project manager? Is it both and more? The studies that have focused on project success have an inherent flaw, in that they are based on the subjective view of the people who participated in the case study. A specific group of stakeholders may have a strong view of why a particular project was a success, but the project manager may have a completely different view; both may be right or both may be wrong. Can research in this area identify a different view, perspective, or methodology to be applied to academic analysis of project outcomes to reduce the subjectivity in the definition of project success?

(continued)

3. The increased focus on the people side of projects has been a key feature of the academic literature. However, the contribution of change management to the overall success of projects has not been widely researched. Empirical academic study is needed to substantiate the industry-based studies such as Prosci (2012) to quantify the impact that change management has had on project success.

This section has reviewed the principles associated with project success, highlighting the key factors that studies have presented to align projects with successful outcomes. The literature has emphasized the importance of an increased focus on the people side of project management as part of the overall project CSFs. A framework for the categorization of success has been presented to illustrate some of many facets of success. The section has highlighted the problems some organizations have encountered in defining success and the importance of defining success criteria at the beginning of the project.

Summary of Key Points

- Project success is a complex and multifaceted concept.
- Defining success criteria at the start of the project can mitigate the risk of not agreeing success during implementation.
- CSFs have evolved from the traditional technical aspects to include people-related factors that represent adoption and benefits realization.
- Pinpointing the exact reasons for the success of a project is inherently subjective in that the success factors are the product of stakeholder opinion.
- Studies have attached an equal weighting between soft skills and the traditional technical skills of project managers in the context of delivering successful projects.
- Project success is more likely if the sponsor is engaged with the project and visible to the stakeholders.
- Organizations must be wary of assuming that the adoption of a specific methodology will result in project success.

Chapter 4 presents the processes and practices undertaken in the management of projects and the performance aspects of project management. Methodology and standards are also included as are the actualities of delivering projects in the real world.

Chapter 4
Project Management Processes and Practice

In the last section, we covered the issues in contextualizing project success and some of the key critical success factors that have been presented in the literature. We now turn our attention to project management and highlight some of the key areas in standards, performance, and approach. The initial section of this section describes two of the main standards used for the management of IS projects in particular the PMBoK® and PRINCE2®. The key contents of both standards are discussed in terms of content and performance based on the available literature. The section then progresses to discuss the actualities of project management and some of the complexities of project delivery.

4.1 Project Standards and the Body of Knowledge

The practitioner guidance on the definition of a project has been described as a temporary endeavor undertaken to create a unique product, service, or result, framed by a defined beginning and end date (OGC Group 2013; Project Management Institute 2014). Whereas project management is defined as the planning, delegation, monitoring, and control of the project to achieve the defined objectives within the constraints of time, cost, quality, scope, benefits, and risk (OGC Group 2013; Project Management Institute 2014). These definitions have been subject to slight variation in the academic literature, but the basic premise of a temporary organization created to deliver a product or products and the formal management of that delivery to defined success criteria runs through most of the definitions.

The main formal structured project management standards used by organizations for the management of projects are PRINCE2® and PMBoK®. The Association for Project Management (APM) also publishes a Body of Knowledge (BoK) that supports mainly UK-based project managers, but for the purposes of this book, we will make reference to the Project Management Institute published PMBoK®. The Office for Government and Commerce (OGC) in the UK is responsible for the development

© The Author(s) 2016
D.L. Hughes et al., *Success and Failure of IS/IT Projects*,
SpringerBriefs in Information Systems, DOI 10.1007/978-3-319-23000-9_4

and ongoing improvements to PRINCE2® with input from outside contributors from academia and industry. The practitioner accreditation function is performed by Accrediting Professional Managers Globally (APMG). The PMBoK® is developed and published by the PMI and is positioned as the global standard for project management. An agile approach to the management of projects (Agile Project Management) has recently emerged from the collaboration between the APMG and the Dynamic Systems Development Method (DSDM) consortium. The method is positioned as a standard that embraces the iterative benefits of an agile approach with adequate levels of structure to provide management control and oversight. This new standard is positioned as either a stand-alone method or one that can work alongside standards such as PRINCE2®, but to date there is little academic analysis of the approach to gauge its effectiveness in the delivery of successful projects.

PRINCE2® is structured around four integrated elements: *principles*, *themes*, *processes*, and the *tailoring* of the method. The *principles* set out a framework of best practice for the project, the *themes* describe the integrated aspects of the project that must be continually addressed throughout the project, the *processes* are a set of activities that need to be incorporated to direct, manage, and deliver a project, and *tailoring* is the flexible application of the method. The concept surrounding the mandatory use of the PRINCE2® *principles* is the provision of a framework that project managers follow while being pragmatic in the application of the method so as not to get caught up with high levels of process and documentation on projects that do not require it. For a project to be described as a PRINCE2® project, all of the seven principles must be employed (OGC Group 2013).

The seven PRINCE2® *principles* listed within (OGC Group 2013) highlight:

- *Continued Business Justification*: importance of not embarking on a project that does not have a business case and for the business case to be valid throughout the project.
- *Learn from Experience*: learning the lessons from previous projects.
- *Defined Roles and Responsibilities*: formal definition of roles and responsibilities for the key stakeholder groupings of business, user, and supplier.
- *Manage by Stages*: management and planning of the project by stages to provide greater control and ease of monitoring.
- *Manage by Exception*: management by exception within predefined limits of tolerance to enable appropriate governance without micromanaging of the project by the organization executive.
- *Focus on Products*: focus on product delivery to agreed quality rather than activity-oriented tasks.
- *Tailor to Suit the Project Environment*: tailoring of the method to suit the organizations and projects needs.

The PRINCE2® *themes* of *business case, organization, quality, plans, risk, change*, and *progress* are positioned as the aspects of project management that must be addressed continually throughout the project. All seven themes must be applied in a PRINCE2® project, but need to be tailored to suit the complexity and scale of the project. The emphasis on the importance of the business case is a key principle of the

PRINCE2® standard ensuring that the project manager and the project executive revisit the justification and defined benefits periodically throughout the project at the end of each management stage. Each of the *themes* has a number of products (tangible outputs or deliverables) with responsibilities for creation and monitoring relevant to project role. PRINCE2® *processes* detail the set of activities to direct, manage, and deliver a project based on defined inputs and outputs (OGC Group 2013).

Each of the PRINCE2® *processes* listed within (OGC Group 2013) from *starting a project* through to the final *closing a project* details the objective, purpose, and responsibilities for producing and maintaining each of the deliverables at each stage of the project. The processes are separated into three levels of control processes: *directing*, *managing*, and *delivering* and four project life-cycle processes: *starting up a project*, *initiating a project*, *managing a stage boundary*, and *closing a project*:

- *Stating up a project*: ascertaining if the project is worthwhile with a clear business justification.
- *Directing a project*: governance and authorization responsibilities of the project board ensuring accountability is in place while delegating day-to-day management of the project to the project manager.
- *Initiating a project*: develop the understanding required to quantify the work that needs to be done to deliver the required products before committing to significant spend.
- *Controlling a stage*: project management responsibilities for the work required for the stage within agreed tolerance limits.
- *Managing product delivery*: responsibilities for the creation and delivery of the defined products coordinated by the team manager and reporting to the project manager.
- *Managing a stage boundary*: executed toward the end of each management stage to ensure the project board has sufficient information to review the current stage progress and authorize the next stage.
- *Closing a project*: defines a clear end to the project and formalizes a review point in the context of benefits and verification of acceptance of project.

The *tailoring* aspects of the PRINCE2® refer to the adaptation and application of the method on large and small projects to suit the environment of the organization, while attempting to continue providing appropriate levels of control and governance. The guidance warns of the inappropriate tailoring of the method where key elements are omitted, leading to a flawed implementation of PRINCE2® (OGC Group 2013). Organizations that implement PRINCE2®, but do not tailor the method appropriately, risk initiating an overburdened, overmanaged project. The key ethos behind the *tailoring* of the method is that each of the PRINCE2® *principles* and *themes* must be implemented, but the adaptation can be adjusted to suit the project size and scope. The guidance gives some examples of tailoring, i.e., oral reports to the project board, email instead of formal reports, skipping the creation of the project brief, project manager undertaking the role of project support and team member, and simplified business case that includes project justification (OGC Group 2013).

The PRINCE2® guidance within (OGC Group 2013) includes a disclaimer that it does not cover all aspects of project management highlighting that a number of areas are deliberately considered to be out of scope:

- *Specialist products*: this includes procurement, organizational change management, software development methods and standards, and test management methods.
- *Detailed techniques*: planning and control techniques, e.g., earned value and critical path analysis.
- *Leadership capability*: style and motivational aspects of leadership.

Although not explicitly referenced in the PRINCE2® text, the guidance also excludes any contract or financial management aspects, cultural issues within the organization, political, and user adoption factors (OGC Group 2013). The framing of these exclusions can be considered from different perspectives depending on how PRINCE2® is viewed and the experience of the practitioner or organization that intends to utilize the method. It could be argued that excluding these elements is reasonable, in that it is unrealistic to expect the method to cover all areas of project management. However, a different view is that organizations choose a method such as PRINCE2® to help them deliver successful projects. If the method deliberately excludes key areas such as change management, leadership style, interpersonal skills, and so on, then the method could be described as incomplete.

PRINCE2® advocates the analysis of and engagement with stakeholders. The guidance includes some basic elements of change management within the *organization* theme as part of the *communications management strategy,* produced during project initiation. The product defines the communication needs for the project and the means and frequency of the communication (OGC Group 2013). However, the guidance also references stakeholders in the context of analyzing resistance, i.e., stakeholders who see the project as a threat, those who support or oppose the project, and those users who can act as blockers to the project and its progress (OGC Group 2013). Therefore, PRINCE2® recognizes the importance of stakeholder analysis and communication providing some high-level guidance. However, it fails to provide any detail on mitigating or managing user resistance and omits any reference to direct the practitioner to a suitable change management method for more specialized guidance. It is not clear from the PRINCE2® standard where the boundary lines are in terms of what is in and out of scope. It is unclear at what stage the practitioner needs to look elsewhere for more specific guidance for the areas not covered by PRINCE2®. Furthermore, in the context of project failure, specifically UK public sector IS failure, studies have shown that projects have failed for a number of reasons (Bronte-Stuart 2009), many of which are the areas specifically excluded from PRINCE2®. Assuming that the majority of these IS failures are PRINCE2® projects (PRINCE2® is mandated for UK public sector projects), this suggests a gap exists in either the content of the method or how it is applied. A thorough and successful application of the PRINCE2® standard on a failed IS project will still be judged as a failure regardless of the reasons for failure and whether those reasons are excluded from the standard.

The fifth edition of the PMBoK® is structured around a list of ten knowledge areas and five process groups that are centered on the concept of *good practice* in the context of application of knowledge, skills, tools, and techniques developed to increase the likelihood of project success (Project Management Institute 2014). The five PMBoK® process groups are *initiating, planning, executing, monitoring and control, and closing.* Each of the processes is positioned as a set of interrelated actions and activities with inputs and outputs that are required to create a specified product, service, or result. Project processes generally fall within the two major categories of *project management-based* processes and *product-oriented* processes. The former deals with the skills and capabilities required for the knowledge areas and the latter describes the details surrounding product creation and delivery. The process groups are linked via the outputs they produce to form a project lifecycle spanning the start and end of a project. The process groups are not intended to be aligned with the project lifecycle but would normally be repeated for each of the standard life-cycle phases such as feasibility, design, or test (Project Management Institute 2014).

The PMBoK® knowledge areas within (Project Management Institute 2014) are:

- *Project integration management*: the management of the interdependencies between the various processes and activities that form the project management process groups.
- *Project scope management*: processes to control the requirements and subsequent work required to successfully complete the project. When the project scope is baselined, all subsequent changes will be carried out under formal change control.
- *Project time management:* processes required to complete the project within the agreed time constraints.
- *Project cost management*: processes that manage the planning estimation and control of project costs and agreed budget.
- *Project quality management*: processes that define, control, and validate the quality aspects of the projects deliverables.
- *Project human resources management*: processes that identify, organize, and manage the project team and its performance.
- *Project communication management*: processes for the identification, planning, and control of appropriate and effective stakeholder communications on the project.
- *Project risk management*: processes for the identification, quantifying, and management of risks on the project.
- *Project procurement management:* processes for the purchase of products and services required by the project to include any subsequent contract management directly linked to the procurement activity.
- *Project stakeholders management*: processes for the identification, engagement, and management of stakeholders that could be impacted by the project. Includes the management of any resistance and adoption issues.

Each of the knowledge areas has a matrix relationship with the process groups for the definition of specific processes. For example, the project scope management knowledge area covers the process: 5.1 plan scope management and the process: 5.2 collect requirements. These two processes have a matrix relationship to the planning process group. The complete set of the 47 PMBoK® processes follow the same format and are aligned with the relevant knowledge areas and process group (Project Management Institute 2014).

The PMBoK® is not prescriptive, in that it is not designed to provide the project manager with a step-by-step methodology to manage a project. The standard is structured around a number of key knowledge areas and relies on the project manager to define or apply a suitable set of processes or method to provide structure to the project (Project Management Institute 2014). The PMBoK® specifically excludes guidance on project portfolio management and program management, but identifies the key texts to consult for further guidance on these two areas. The PMBoK® positions itself as a *good practice* guide for project managers and not a methodology, highlighting that methodologies such as PRINCE2®, agile, or other approaches can be used (Project Management Institute 2014). However, there are difficulties with this, in that PRINCE2® and PMBoK® use different terminology in a number of areas, i.e., *project initiation document* and *stages*—PRINCE2®, *project charter* and *phases*—PMBoK®. The standards also overlap each other with alternative approaches to project organization structure, emphasis on key role of business case, governance, and approaches to stakeholder management. It is not clear from the practitioner perspective on where the PMBoK® guidance ends and where the project manager needs to look elsewhere for a more detailed information on key sections of the project. The project stakeholder management knowledge area within the PMBoK® references key change management aspects such as building trust, resolving conflict, active listening, and overcoming resistance to change (Project Management Institute 2014). However, the standard does not provide the necessary detail to formally manage these aspects. The PMBoK® would perhaps better serve the needs of practitioners by explicitly referencing external guidance on topics such as the complexities of user resistance, allocation of resources for change management in the context of ROI, organizational change maturity, user adoption, and sustaining the change brought about by project implementation.

4.2   Project Methodology and Project Performance

The analysis of project management standards and specific methodological approaches in the context of contribution to successful project outcomes has largely been omitted from the literature. The lack of academic focus on PRINCE2® in particular is surprising given that it is the standard mandated for most UK public sector IS projects and that the literature highlights numerous large public sector IS failures over many years (Beynon-Davies 1995; Fitzgerald and Russo 2005; McGrath 2002; Warne and Hart 1997). PRINCE2® has been criticized by practitioners for the weaknesses of its risk management process, lacking sufficient detail in the estimation and impact of project risk (Elkington and Smallman 2002). Studies have also criticized the unwieldy nature of PRINCE2® and its overreliance on high levels of documentation (White and Fortune 2002), although the standard attempts to mitigate this by emphasizing the importance of tailoring the method to suit the application.

The failed projects analyzed in Avison and Wilson (2002) and Beynon-Davies (1995) have highlighted that either no formal methodology was applied, or one was used but not applied correctly. The root cause analysis of the project failures outlined by Gauld (2007), Mitev (1996), Pan et al. (2008), and Verner and Abdullah (2012) implicitly references the characteristics of a project management methodology but omit any discussion on the application of standards or methods. Agile methods are referenced in Standish Group (2013), but only in the context of running small projects to potentially deliver in shorter timescales. Specific aspects of project management methodology are referenced in some studies (Dwivedi et al. 2013b; Heeks 2002; Keider 1974; Nelson 2007), i.e., risk management, requirements management, and user resistance. However, these studies omit to reference a formal methodological approach to project management or application of project management standards. The public sector project failure as outlined by Warne and Hart (1997) highlighted that modern project management techniques were used on the project, yet failure still occurred. The study omits to indicate if the standard itself was the problem or the expertise of the project management team was at fault in the application of the standard. Poor project management is a frequently cited failure factor. It is listed in a number of studies of IS failure (Brown and Jones 1998; Emam and Koru 2008; Gauld 2007; Keil et al. 1998; Nawi et al. 2011; Pan et al. 2008). However, studies omit to indicate if these failings are methodology based in terms of how the methodology was applied or if the failings were a direct result of the project manager not undertaking his or her duties effectively. This is a key point in terms of the direction of further academic research, in that failure could be a direct result of the method itself and its suitability for the project therefore, highlighting perhaps some key gaps in the standard. Alternatively, the personality, leadership, or ability of the project manager could be a significant factor behind the failure regardless of the method used.

It is assumed that organizations adopting a formal project management methodology do so, with the expectation that this will increase the chances of project success. However, if the adherence to standards yields only negligible results, organizations must question their commitment and investment in project management methods and standards (Crawford 2005). The push toward the greater professionalizing of the industry over the last three decades, driven by the main project management standards bodies, does not seem to have had a dramatic impact on the successful outcomes of large complex IS projects (Standish Group 2013). The link between project management standards and successful project outcomes is an under-researched area requiring further academic analysis to quantify the contribution from the adoption of formal project management methods. Additionally, the claims of ease of integration of PRINCE2® and agile within PMBoK® and agile with PRINCE2® as a unified method to better assure successful outcomes are yet to be conclusively tested via academic study.

4.3   The Actualities of Project Management and Delivery

The literature has historically omitted to focus much attention on the everyday experiences of project managers attempting to deliver projects within industry—the so-called *actuality of projects*. Projects are inherently complex, not just in the technical sense, but in the context of differing social constructs as well as their political and organizational focus within an organization. Project actuality emphasizes an understanding of the lived experience of people involved with projects encompassing a real-world view of the decisions and behaviors that are subject to continuous change (Cicmil et al. 2006). The key aims for the detailed analysis of project actuality are to provide a new perspective, and an alternative account of what project managers do in real-life project situations, and to explore the skills and knowledge of practitioners in action (Cicmil et al. 2006). Insights from the practitioner perspective can provide feedback on the practical aspects of implementing formal standards, methods, frameworks, or models and the applicability or limitations of academic theorization (Winter et al. 2006a). There is a tangible gap between the narrative-based frameworks, models, bodies of knowledge, and standards in project management and the implementation environment of real people working within a mixed social and cultural organization with political constraints and complexities.

Formal project management has now become the dominant model within industry for strategic implementation, business improvement, and transformation projects. Nonetheless, the conceptual base of project management has been criticized for its lack of relevance to practice (Cooke-Davies 2002; Kloppenborg and Opfer 2002). The Rethinking Project Management (RPM) initiative was formed to address the growing critique that project management required a new perspective to incorporate other disciplines to enrich and extend the field beyond its current intellectual foundations (Winter et al. 2006a). At its onset the RPM network attracted academics from 15 universities around the world together with senior practitioners from the public and private sectors aiming to create an interdisciplinary network of academics, researchers, and practitioners interested in developing the field of project management and extending the body of research beyond its current foundations. The RPM network developed a list of key topics that formed the agreed basis for directions for future research (Winter et al. 2006a):

- *Life-cycle model of projects and PM* toward *theories of the complexity of projects and PM*—the need for multiple images to inform and guide action at all levels in the management of projects rather than a reliance on the classic life-cycle model.
- *Projects as instrumental processes* toward *projects as social processes*—moving from the traditional sequence of production-oriented tasks to be performed to a project that focuses on social interaction among people taking account of the social agenda and practices stakeholder relations, politics, and power.
- *Product creation as the prime focus* toward value *creation*—the temporary production or improvement to a product leading toward concepts and frameworks where value creation is the key factor.

- *Narrow conceptualization of projects toward a broader conceptualization of projects*—moving away from concepts and methodologies that start from a well-defined objective toward an approach that facilitates a broader conceptualization of projects acknowledging the multidisciplinary nature and multiple purposes of projects where the scope is not always predefined.
- *Practitioners as trained technicians toward practitioners as reflective practitioners*—where practitioners have traditionally followed detailed procedures prescribed by project management methods toward a culture of developing reflective practitioners who can learn and adapt effectively in complex project environments through experience, intuition, and application of theory in practice.

Key Points for Practitioners

- Learn the lessons from past projects; most if not all of the issues that may affect your project will have occurred before.
- Expect changes to requirements and plan for them especially on long lead-time projects.
- The application of a selected set of standards, methodology, or body of knowledge by itself cannot guarantee success. Look outside of the method and incorporate the necessary aspects that are not included.
- Tailor the selected method to suit the context of the project within the organization.
- Look beyond the traditional elements of time, costs, and quality to include more of the *soft skills* elements that can make the difference between success and failure.
- The reality of managing projects extends far beyond the standards guidance or the training manual. Don't underestimate the contribution of experience.
- Other factors that are outside of the conventional project management sphere of influence can have a significant impact on outcomes. Political, cultural, and social issues may affect the project and can't be ignored.

Winter et al. (2006a, b) contextualized the reflective practitioner concept by highlighting that project managers need to operate effectively in the so-called *swampy lowlands* of projects and that current training and development tends to center on particular products such as PRINCE2® rather than emphasizing the role of people in project success. Cicmil et al. (2006) hypothesized that a better understanding of project actuality and the complex social processes that occur at various levels of project working could enhance the intellectual foundations of the project management field. The study characterized actuality research as focusing on *social process* and how practitioners think in action considering issues such as complexity, power, intuition, decision-making collaborative working, learning and communication, and the relationship between agency and structure in the local context (Cicmil et al. 2006). Researching the actuality of projects entails the collecting, analyzing, and disseminating of knowledge about people working in the project environment and their interaction with technologies, processes, methods, and each other (Winter et al. 2006a).

The pressures inherent within the project environment especially in the context of large and complex projects with numerous elements and interdependencies within multifaceted organizations highlight the high levels of uncertainty that project managers are faced with in the delivery of change in organizations. The conventional approach of applying project bodies of knowledge and formal methodologies to the management of projects is by no means a guarantee of success (Crawford 2005), indicating that other factors are influential on outcomes. These factors may be political, environmental, technical, or cultural in nature and perhaps reflect an actuality fact that the early phase eliciting of requirements and planning are inherently fallible and do not reflect the natural emergence of projects in the real world (Cicmil et al. 2006). Future success relies on project managers looking outside the structure of the chosen project methodology to develop an understanding of how to contextualize the approach to cater for the actualities of the project.

This section has highlighted a number of areas in the literature that would benefit from further academic research. The key topics are outlined in the highlighted box below:

Recommendations for Future Research

1. The PRINCE2® method does not provide any guidance outside of the time, cost, and quality criteria omitting any people, leadership, or cultural aspects to project delivery. How do project managers bridge the gap in delivering successful projects? Is PRINCE2® supplemented with any specific practices or methods that have been shown to complement the method and support the elements not catered for in the delivery of successful outcomes? Research into these practices could yield valuable information on how the method is applied in practice.
2. The PMBoK® references the applicability of the guidance to be integrated with PRINCE2® or agile-based methods, but how successful is this in practice? How do project managers deal with the different use of terminology and the numerous overlaps in guidance?
3. The conventional approach of applying project bodies of knowledge and formal methodologies to the management of projects does not necessarily translate to a successful project (Crawford 2005). Why is this the case? Is the wrong method used or is it how the method was applied?
4. Studies have hypothesized that a better understanding of project actuality and the complex social processes can enhance the intellectual foundations of project management (Cicmil et al. 2006), yet the training of practitioners omits many of these areas. Further research in this area could help to build a case for proposing a more rounded realistic practitioner path that reflects what really takes place within projects.

This section has detailed the key components of project management and highlighted the use of standards and the performance aspects of project managers in delivering projects. The practicalities of managing projects are also covered in the context of highlighting the actualities of delivering projects within organizations.

Summary of Key Points

- De facto project management standards do not contain all the guidance required to deliver a successful project.
- Conventional project management has been criticized in some studies for its lack of relevance to what actually happens on the ground within organizations.
- The actuality of projects is a key area of research providing insights into the practical application of project management standards.
- Large and complex projects with numerous elements and interdependencies within multifaceted organizations highlight the uncertainty that project managers are faced with in the delivery of change within organizations.
- Project managers need to have the skills to operate effectively in a multitude of environments that requires a skillset that exceeds the current training and development requirements.

Chapter 5 explores the discipline of change management and outlines how issues stemming from user resistance can result in poor adoption and the inability of projects to deliver their full benefits. Project managers cannot ignore change management and need to understand its key concepts to apply the principles on their projects.

Chapter 5
Change Management

In the previous section, we discussed some of the methodological aspects of managing projects, highlighting that project managers need to look beyond the prescribed standards to deal with the complexities of delivering projects. This section describes the background and key processes that underpin change management. The concept of change management has been introduced in previous sections in the context of project success and failure. Here we progress in greater detail to discuss the underlying principles and application. The narrative starts by defining the commonly cited change models and then moving on to describe the impacts of resistance to change and sustaining change within organizations. This theme continues with an examination of the practicalities of managing change in reality and the importance of engaging effectively with stakeholders. The section ends with a discussion of the ROI issues faced by managers seeking to procure change management resource on projects.

5.1 Change Models and the Change Process

Change Management has been defined as "*the application of a structured process and set of tools for leading the people side of change to achieve a desired outcome*" (Prosci 2012, p. 88) and "*the process of continually reviewing an organization's direction, structure and capabilities to serve the ever changing needs of internal and external customers*" (Moran and Brightman 2000). Hiatt and Creasey (2012) posed the question why change management? The authors highlighted the issues of change in the workplace in terms of a new process or new technology, with staff failing to embrace change leading to little value or benefit realization to the organization. By following a structured approach to change management, users are better able to accept change, thereby enabling organizations to realize their business objectives (Hiatt and Creasey 2012). For change to succeed, organizations must recognize the importance of users understanding the internal and external drivers for change and how the change initiative fits into the bigger picture of why the change is needed (Change Management Institute 2013).

© The Author(s) 2016

D.L. Hughes et al., *Success and Failure of IS/IT Projects*,
SpringerBriefs in Information Systems, DOI 10.1007/978-3-319-23000-9_5

A change initiative has a low chance of success if organizations are not *change ready*. The energy required to initiate change and the capabilities that underpin it cannot be conjured up over a short period of time through the pulling of a single lever (Pettigrew et al. 1992). Luecke (2003) identified three characteristics of change readiness: *organization has effective and respected leaders, people in the organization are personally motivated to change, and the organization has a non-hierarchical structure*. Luecke (2003) highlighted four suggestions to make an organization better prepared for change: *Undertake a unit by unit change readiness assessment, develop more participative approaches to how everyday business is handled, give people a voice, and drive out fear*. Hiatt and Creasey (2012) developed a three-phase process for organizational change management: *preparing for change, managing change*, and *reinforcing change* highlighting the initial phase activities of identifying the scope of the change and key aspects of ensuring the readiness of the organization to embark on the change programme. Management within organizations need to build a climate for change that justifies why the change is needed, raise energy levels, and build the capability to mount the change (Pettigrew and Whipp 1993).

Various models and frameworks have been proposed within the body of literature to attempt to provide a structure and process for the formal management of change. The *unfreeze, move*, and *refreeze* components of the widely cited Lewin's three-step model (Lewin 1951) highlight a structured change process but is viewed as somewhat simplistic in the modern era, lacking detail on sustaining change and assuming that change can be permanent. The four-stage model of change developed by Bullock and Batten (1985) highlights phases of planned change: *exploration, planning, action*, and *integration*, emphasizing the need to align the change with other areas of the organization. The model is limited by its somewhat technical nature and lack of focus on resistance. Beckhard and Harris (1987) proposed a simplistic formulaic approach to assess readiness for change, highlighting potential gaps and identify barriers to change. However, although the change formula is adept at describing the process of change, the method has been criticized for the potential difference in approach in the use of the formula and its potential to deliver varying outcomes (Cameron and Green 2012).

The change models as outlined in Carnall (1990) and Bridges (1991) emphasize the complexity of the transition elements of change. They identified the challenge of managing the inherent physiological factors and key aspects of utilizing managers who are skilled in managing the change transition process. The eight-step model proposed by Kotter (1995) has been widely cited in the literature and emphasizes the importance of allocating significant up-front effort and resources for the change. The eight steps in the model comprise: *Establish a sense of urgency, Form a powerful guiding coalition, Create a vision, Communicate the vision, Empower others to act on the vision, Plan for and creating short-term wins, Consolidating improvements and producing still more change, Institutionalizing new approaches* (Kotter 1995). Kotter (1995) also recognized that unless an early, critical level of inertia is developed and actively supported by the executive and senior management team, change is unlikely to succeed.

The approach to the change management process taken by Senge et al. (1999) deviates from the bulk of the literature in that they advocate approaching change from a perspective of starting small, growing steadily, expecting challenges along the way, and not attempting to plan the change initiative in detail as an up-front exercise. Senge describes change as a natural human growth process rather than a mechanistic and formulaic path and highlights the importance of managers understanding the likely setbacks and the longer-term issues of sustaining change (Senge et al. 1999). The ADKAR change model as outlined in Hiatt and Creasey (2012) emphasizes the importance of planning, managing, and reinforcing change from the people perspective. The ADKAR acronym, *Awareness, Desire, Knowledge, Ability,* and *Reinforcement* (Hiatt and Creasey 2012), forms the basis of managing individual change within an organization. The model is sequential and cumulative, in that individuals must progress from a starting point of being aware of the required change through to actively reinforcing the change at the end of the process. ADKAR has been criticized for focusing on process instead of people as well as failing to fully distinguish between individual and organizational change (Hornstein 2015). However, Hiatt and Creasey (2012) clearly detail the complexities of change emphasizing the importance of analyzing and managing the resistance of individuals and the Prosci® change methodology that ADKAR sits within includes a detailed process for organizational change management. The Change Management Body of Knowledge (CMBoK) is positioned as a recognized standard for practicing change managers. The guidance describes the knowledge that underpins change management practice and is based on 8 years of Change Management Institute (CMI) research and the experiences of 600 practitioners in 30 countries. The guidance includes 13 separate knowledge areas and a change model based around organizational maturity in *project change management, business change readiness,* and *organizational change leadership.* The CMBoK could be seen as being somewhat limited to practitioners in that it is not positioned as a detailed step-by-step guide to managing a change initiative requiring further more detailed methodological guidance to manage the actualities of change.

5.2 Impacts of Resistance to Change

Poor change management and resistance to change have been cited in many studies as contributory factors in the failure of IS projects. Studies highlight poor communication of changed processes, lack of user involvement, absence of change management methodology, and user resistance issues as key factors (Barker and Frolick 2003; Hirschheim and Newman 1988; Keil et al. 1998). High-profile project failures such as the LASCAD project and the SNCF Socrate project have been extensively analyzed in the literature highlighting problems due to lack of user engagement and poor change management with project management concentrating on the technical aspects of the project and failing to mitigate user resistance issues (Beynon-Davies 1995; Fitzgerald and Russo 2005; McGrath 2002; Mitev 1996). Project managers have been shown to underestimate the complexities of user resistance and to fully appreciate the social and political nature of organizational change (Hirschheim and Newman 1988).

Attempts to deliver significant change to an organization are liable to generate unintended consequences, unforeseen implications, unpredictable ripple effects, and arguments from those who anticipate a sense of loss from the revised arrangements (Doyle et al. 2000). This sense of loss has been contextualized in studies as an association with grief where humans travel through stages of *denial, bargaining, depression*, and *acceptance* (Kübler-Ross 1973). The anxiety from employees confronted with change can lead to resistance where users are faced with learning something new or the pressure to change (Schein 1992). Nonetheless, this behavior should be seen as normal within organizations, requiring managers to build resistance mitigation and management measures into their plans. Users' resistance behaviors can be variable and highly complex, often based on the personality of the individual and the context in which the change occurs. Factors such as employee skepticism, job security impact, affects on power and prestige, trust in management ability, and the negative reaction from users to the increased amount of information communicated are examples of factors that can have a direct impact on resistance levels (Oreg 2003, 2006; Stanley et al. 2005). Managers need to analyze the underlying reasons for the resistant behavior, understand its origins and its cultural context, and then take steps to reduce it and secure subsequent commitment from stakeholders (Beckhard and Harris 1987; Cameron and Green 2012; Hiatt and Creasey 2012).

Resistance and the natural negative human reactions to change are not regarded in the best practice literature as normal or anticipated components of effective change (Doyle et al. 2000). Resistance is not explicitly addressed within the de facto project management guidance, although it could be argued that the PRINCE2® themes of *risk* and *change* are mechanisms that could be used to highlight resistance issues and manage the risks to the project from user resistance. However, aside from identifying stakeholder communication requirements, the PRINCE2® methodology fails to offer any guidance or processes on the identification and management of resistance at any stage of the project lifecycle. The PMBoK® includes a reference to *overcoming resistance to change* and emphasizing *active management of stakeholder involvement* within its managing stakeholder engagement section, but omits to offer any detailed guidance on how to analyze and deal with individual resistance. These omissions could have unintended consequences during later life-cycle activities where communication, planning, and product delivery could be affected by unresolved user resistance issues as has been highlighted in previous studies on the causes of IS failure (Beynon-Davies 1995; Fitzgerald and Russo 2005; McGrath 2002; Mitev 1996).

5.3 Sustaining Change

The successful implementation of a change initiative is not measured by the initial results of delivery but by the sustained transformation and full delivery of benefits within the organization (Buchanan et al. 2005). This implies an acceptable level of compliance with the processes, system, or working practices at a level where the benefits of the change are realized. The process of sustaining change is dependent on multiple factors interacting on different levels of analysis and time frames (Buchanan et al. 2005). Sustaining change requires a fundamental shift in thinking, requiring an understanding of the forces and challenges that impede progress and workable strategies for dealing with these complexities (Senge et al. 1999). Kotter (1995) references the importance of sustaining change within his eight-step model in the context of consolidating improvements and institutionalizing new approaches emphasizing that change must become part of corporate culture. Kotter (1995) also highlights the consequences of failing to *anchor* change identifying that until new behaviors are rooted in social norms and shared values, they are subject to degradation as soon as the pressure for change is removed. Users affected by change need to be given time to adjust and assess and reflect on the lessons of change in order to consolidate the organizational changes that have been implemented (Doyle et al. 2000). The extensively cited study of change within the UK NHS carried out by Pettigrew et al. (1992) highlights the importance of sustaining the inertia of the change effort and the debilitating effects of regression where permanent change fails to take hold. To mitigate these effects, Pettigrew et al. (1992) recommend that organizations ensure that key change leaders stay in position long enough to see through the change process. The economic reality however in many organizations is that key staff are often reassigned to new projects as the existing projects are wound down through delivery and closure.

The CMBoK proposes that change must be reinforced across the organization to ensure that new behaviors and practices become an intrinsic part of normal operations. The guidance highlights that successful sustained change requires continued monitoring and evaluation of progress to ensure sustaining systems remain effective (Change Management Institute 2013). Aside from advocating monitoring and instigating feedback channels, the CMBoK guidance within this particular knowledge area lacks detail, offering little in terms of any structured process or formal method to ensure change is sustained within organizations. Hiatt and Creasey (2012) include a *Reinforcing Change* phase in their Prosci® Change Management Process that includes *collect and analyze feedback, diagnose gaps and manage resistance, implement corrective actions, and celebrate successes.* Hiatt and Creasey (2012) highlight that one of the biggest mistakes made by change management teams is the omission of reinforcement actions resulting in the same types of failure that stem from not implementing any change management at all within the organization (Hiatt and Creasey 2012).

5.4 Change in Practice

Change is a difficult and emotive concept for many individuals and organizations requiring leaders to think carefully about how to approach change in a planned and organized way. The effective management of the change aspects of any project requires a set of skills and expertise that sits outside the curriculum vitae of many traditional project managers, perhaps reflecting a gap in the training and learning curve of practitioners supported by the lack of change management content in the project bodies of knowledge and standards guidance. The attributes expected of good project managers, namely, leadership and organizational skills, articulation of clear direction, numeracy, and analytical ability, do not fit the profile of individuals who are able to steer organizations through periods of change. Cameron and Green (2012) highlighted the requirement for new leadership skills and practices and developed a set of attributes required for leading significant change:

- *Presence and deep listening*—looking beyond our preconceptions and historical ways of making sense and allowing leaders to operate from a deeper sense of purpose and discard old identities. Trying to really hear what people are trying to say to fully appreciate the different perspectives.
- *The importance of framing*—the ability for management to paint a picture that illustrates the change destination, and the holding of this frame in a clear and consistent way for others to engage with it and complete the picture. The framing aspect of change can also mean setting out the broad phases of change with the key milestones so stakeholders can gain a tangible sense of how the process will feel. Reframing may be appropriate where the change is being viewed in an unhelpful way and obstacles arise.
- *Developing the capacity to contain*—containment in the context of change means providing a holding environment for anxieties and other pressure-related emotions, so they can be worked through in a calm structured way. In the heat of a change project, it is key to give stakeholders the opportunity to articulate problems within an environment that facilitates this rather than the project team having to react to issues and rumors on the back foot. From the leadership perspective, containment means finding ways of acknowledging and empathizing with people's anxieties and emotions rather than suppressing them.
- *Negative capability*—ability to provide support to teams in their task of preventing habitual patterns of working or falling back on existing working practices. Negating can allow the creative process to follow its own course and prevent premature closure of ideas and initiatives. It can be a fine line between leaders actively intervening by rolling up their sleeves to push through change and deliberately holding off from active intervention and to trust the process.
- *Practicing self-care*—leaders involved in stressful, long drawn out change projects where the task at hand becomes all-encompassing, may risk burnout, and end up jeopardizing the project. Taking time out and connecting with other aspects of one's life can enable leaders to better contextualize the problems at hand and see the bigger picture.

Key Points for Practitioners

- Effective stakeholder analysis and assessment of an organization's change maturity and readiness is vital to deliver success.
- Implementing change management practices in the middle or later stages of the project increases the risk of resistance and adoption issues.
- Resistance should be seen as a natural consequence of change and the steps required to mitigate its effects should be planned and suitably resourced.
- The project team needs to be resourced with change ready practitioners that are focused on the change effort and working with the project to deliver its benefits.

Organizations are faced with difficult decisions when contemplating change projects. Executives may be familiar with the concept of a project and the required structure, resources, and terminology, but are perhaps less familiar or comfortable with change management. This can sometimes result in project managers pitching for change management resource with the executive uncertain of the ROI for the allocation of specific additional funds, to what they see as the core project activities. Reminding executives of the poor track record of project delivery especially where poor change management and user resistance are seen to be key factors in their failure (Barker and Frolick 2003; Hirschheim and Newman 1988; Keil et al. 1998) can be a powerful motivator. The consequence of executives not appreciating the importance and role of change management on projects can result in attempts to implement *change management lite* that is likely to result in poor ROI leading to slower acceptance of change within the organization. Formally including change management as part of the early phase initial project risk assessment may be a good opportunity for executives to easily equate the true cost and impact of poorly managed change with the benefits and ROI highlighted in the context of risk mitigation.

The reality in many environments is that change management is not always initiated at the same time as the project. Consequently, teams may find themselves reacting to unforeseen resistance issues and attempting to fire fight on the back foot. Hiatt and Creasey (2012) highlighted these issues and emphasized that the change team needs to be flexible enough to react to several project entry point scenarios:

- *Project start-up*—the project has recently started or is within the planning stage and change management is to be an integral component of the project. This is the best-case scenario and often relies on a change aware project sponsor that can support the timely change effort on the project.
- *Implementation stage*—the project has completed the start-up and design phases of the project and has moved to implementation, requiring change management to be leveraged into existing processes, team structures, and plans.
- *Reaction point entry*—the project has commenced the implementation stage and the project team is already experiencing resistance from users. The net effect of this scenario is an attempt to introduce change management as a reaction to resistance. This is the worst-case scenario.

Each of the above entry points into a project has consequences for the change management effort. The later the entry point in the project the more difficult the task of managing change becomes (Hiatt and Creasey 2012). Additionally, the change management model or method needs to be adaptable to cater for different life-cycle entry points requiring change managers to have a critical understanding of how to apply change management principles in this context (Hiatt and Creasey 2012).

Project and change managers must understand the emotional aspects of change and appreciate the psychological background to resistance behaviours. Change projects are not likely to succeed unless the project engenders a culture where people are receptive to change. Motivating users to move from their natural resistance mind-set requires a hearts and minds effort from the change team, to understand the factors behind human emotion to change. Project teams must identify areas of possible resistance and plan for it. This requires a thorough analysis of the stakeholders, an appreciation of the political and cultural aspects of the organization, and an assessment of the change from the users' perspective (Cameron and Green 2012). By proactively preparing for resistance, project managers are better able to mitigate its effects and move forward and build a coalition for change within the organization (Change Management Institute 2013).

Recommendations for Future Research

1. The decision faced by executives that agree on the importance of change management is how much resource is necessary and what is the ROI. The answer to this question has many aspects. For example, what is the culture of the organization? Are the users change ready? How much change is required from users in order to fully realize the benefits of the new system? The project manager will be unable to answer these questions by referring to the bodies of knowledge or project management methodologies. Can the application of a change maturity model or framework provide these answers? Further research into these aspects could smooth the path in assisting the project manager to secure the required resource to aid effective delivery.
2. Industry-based studies highlight the benefits of reduced resistance and increased ROI if change management is involved early in the lifecycle, ideally at the start of the project. Further research is recommended in this area to validate these claims and to quantify the impacts of diverging from this model.
3. The effectiveness of change management to positively affect project outcomes is an under-researched area. Industry-based studies support this principle, but independent academic study could yield further insight into the details of these claims and highlight the particular aspects that yield the greatest benefits in terms of positive outcomes.

This section has discussed the key concepts and application of change management and highlighted some of the key areas that are faced by organizations embarking on change projects. The formal management of the change process is fundamental to the success of projects and the failure to address the key areas of resistance and user adoption are likely to reduce the chances of success.

Summary of Key Points

- If organizations are not prepared for change or have low levels of change maturity, then the change initiative has a much lower chance of success.
- Project managers have been shown to underestimate the complexities of user resistance and to fully understand the social and political nature of organizational change.

(continued)

- Resistance to change is a normal behavior and should be managed effectively by the project team.
- Change needs to be sustained beyond delivery to ensure the full realization of benefits and failing to reinforce the change can result in failure.
- Leading significant change requires a specific set of attributes that do not fall within the standard project management practitioner framework.
- Early inclusion of change management on a project can lessen the impact of unforeseen events and circumstances later on in the project lifecycle.

Can a more integrated approach to change and project management help to deliver more consistent successful outcomes? This subject is tackled in Chap. 6 where we outline the rationale for organizations to approach change and project management in a more cohesive way to ensure the best chance of success.

Chapter 6
Integration of Change and Project Management

This section discusses the closer integration of change and project management as a mechanism that could add potential benefits to project outcomes. The literature has not focused much attention on this particular topic, but those studies that have addressed this area are analyzed and discussed to develop a case for closer integration. The narrative then describes the potential barriers to the integration of the two areas highlighting the relevant practitioner texts. This section then moves on to highlighting some of the complexities of closer integration and ends with a hypothesis of the potential integrated options.

6.1 The Case for the Integration of Change and Project Management

Although project and change management are mature topics in their own right, with a significant body of research in a range of publications, closer integration of the disciplines and the substantive analysis of the issues and practicalities involved has not received significant focus from the academic community (Söderlund 2011). The inseparability of project and change management has been highlighted in a number of recent studies (Ash 2007; Hornstein 2015; Parker et al. 2013). Ash (2007) theorizes that the two disciplines should not be seen as separate strands or phases of a project with distinct teams but an integral part of the same project. The study analyzed the experiences and feedback from senior project staff who had worked on four separate projects within organizations based in Fiji and Australia. It concludes that the convergence of project and change management is necessary to deliver projects that satisfy stakeholders (Ash 2007). Leyland et al. (2009) asserted that traditional project management fails to recognize the key aspects of change management and investigated the integration of change management concepts with project management in the context of clinical Health Information Technology (HIT)

© The Author(s) 2016

D.L. Hughes et al., *Success and Failure of IS/IT Projects*, SpringerBriefs in Information Systems, DOI 10.1007/978-3-319-23000-9_6 projects. Leyland et al. (2009) emphasize support for the coalescence of project and change management, such that the management of change becomes an essential component in the project management body of knowledge. The study characterizes the relationship between change and project management as an intertwined, mutual co-dependence and highlights that the gap between the two disciplines must be reduced to improve success rates in clinical HIT implementation projects.

Studies that have not explicitly called for greater integration between change and project management have implicitly referenced integration in the context of the project management of organizational change initiatives (Oakland and Tanner 2007; Partington 1996). Söderlund (2011) attempted to advance the debate on change initiatives being organized as projects and the role of project management through the lens of knowledge integration. The study highlighted that the quality of project management becomes decisive for the success of large-scale change processes and that the effectiveness of project management in large-scale change processes is determined by the scope, interdependencies, and speed of the change processes. The findings in Söderlund (2011) highlight the key benefits of organizing change via the mechanisms and process of projects and the contributions to success from the strategic co-location of change and project teams.

Industry-wide benchmarking studies have highlighted how project success is heavily influenced by an organization's approach to structured change management (Prosci 2012). The complexities of user resistance and the omission by project managers to fully understand the social and political nature of organizational change can be key factors in the success (or failure) of IS projects (Hirschheim and Newman 1988). Project management success is as dependent upon people as it is on the technical and functional skills but relies on managers to deliver an integrated approach with joined-up project and change management activities within a unified management plan (Project Management Institute 2014).

6.2 Barriers to Integration

The origins of change and project management highlight quite a different path. Project management has its roots in engineering and construction with practicing managers often rising through the ranks of technical project roles before taking on increasing levels of man management responsibilities. The role of the change manager has its origins in the social sciences and organizational transformation areas. The maturity of project and change management as separate disciplines is also very different with project management demonstrating a track record of nearly five decades with the PMI being created in 1969, but both the CMI and the Association of Change Management Professionals (ACMP) were formed relatively recently in 2004 and 2011, respectively. There were early change management pioneers such as Rogers (1962) who demonstrated the social aspects of consumers adopting new technology, but it took decades for change to be recognized as a key factor within project success and transform into a core discipline of its own.

The concepts, processes, and standards within project and change management are fundamental to the success of any project. However, these two disciplines have separate standards organizations, bodies of knowledge, and practitioner certification paths (Hornstein 2015) with little tangible reference between the two. Both disciplines have their own distinct terminology, use different methods, tools, and techniques, and often have separate organizational structures and reporting lines (Crawford and Hassner-Nahmias 2010). These factors lead to the engendering of an environment where organizations could miss critical dependencies, creating the potential for increased levels of delay, stakeholder miscommunication, and ultimately increased levels of risk on major change projects. These facts are surprising as even a simple analysis of the desired outcomes of both disciplines highlights that each are ultimately created to contribute to and deliver benefits of some form to the organization.

The requirement for an integrated approach to change and project management does not seem to be supported by the key standards—PMBoK® and PRINCE2®, where at best, limited implicit references to change management activities exist. PRINCE2® references stakeholder analysis and engagement within the *organization* theme and *project initiation* process and makes reference to stakeholder communication within *managing stage boundaries* (OGC Group 2013), but the concepts of resistance, individual and organizational change, and sustaining change are not covered. The PMBoK® references stakeholder engagement, stakeholder resistance, and a change management plan as an output of the project stakeholder management knowledge area (Project Management Institute 2014) but fails to address the complexities of planning for and managing high levels of resistance. It also omits the key tasks and processes underpinning the sustaining of change within organizations. On the change management side, the CMBoK guidance extols the virtues of the successful interaction of change and project management. However, it articulates this from a position of silos of expertise and responsibilities, lacking a clear methodology to deliver an integrated approach. The two disciplines each have their own sets of terminology, methodology, and interaction with different parts of the organization (Kotter 1995) potentially providing confusion for the project manager and a barrier to project success. Furthermore, there are numerous instances of overlap between the PMBoK® and CMBoK in terms of CMI knowledge areas and components with the PMBoK® process groups. The net effect of this is the potential for duplicated effort being expended on the assessment of risk, development of plans, and interaction with stakeholders. The CMBoK includes project management as a distinct knowledge area and identifies a set of knowledge components that underpin this. However, although the guidance advocates that the change team should work alongside the project team and for the change plans to be developed in parallel to the project plan (Change Management Institute 2013), there is no attempt to integrate the teams or their activities, thereby implicitly reinforcing the principles of a separate change initiative and project.

Rather than project and change management complementing each other, the two disciplines often end up competing with each other over budgets, roles and responsibilities, access to project sponsors, strategy, and execution. The net effect of these factors can result in one side or the other discounting the contribution from the other with change management often being the discipline that is marginalized or has its budget cut with resulting consequences for successful project outcomes. As each profession has developed its own route to practitioner status and independent standards, the industry has produced a plethora of consulting organizations and proponents of best practice that can advise and assist organizations embarking on major change projects. This leaves executives potentially confused as to which discipline is required to start the initiative and sponsors wondering why they need to procure two sets of competing resource that liaise with the same overlapping group of stakeholders that may end up marginalizing each other (Jarocki 2011).

As a group, project managers have been described as having only moderate skills to manage users and their expectations (Standish Group 2013). Studies have highlighted the different skillsets and training requirements for each of the disciplines. Crawford and Hassner-Nahmias (2010) explored the roles of project and change managers within organizations to gain insight as to which should be managing major transformational change programs. The study asserted that projects and programs that require significant amounts of change demand a high level of interpersonal, astuteness, and sensitivity skills, highlighting a fundamentally different approach to the candid, direct, and rational style valued in competent project mangers (Crawford and Hassner-Nahmias 2010). This view is supported by Cicmil et al. (2006) who asserted that the training in traditional project management discourse may not value the political and social skills necessary to be successful in the complicated and messy real world of projects.

Too often, organizations are structured around separate change and project functions. The net effect of this is a tendency for project managers to abdicate their change management responsibilities to a dedicated change management team and the project sponsor having to procure and manage two sets of resources—a project team and a change team (Kotter 1995; Project Management Institute 2014).

Other fundamental barriers to closer integration include the political and cultural issues within organizations that have been used to separate reporting lines and potentially diverse positions in the organization hierarchy (Jarocki 2011). Reinforcing this view is the reality of the current position of the two disciplines, effectively governed by very separate organizations with their own *raison d'etre* and separate bodies of knowledge with minimal referencing of the other discipline. Each of the main standards organizations has yet to forge any tangible formal interface within their bodies of knowledge leaving practitioners of both disciplines building interactions at various stages of the lifecycle leading to pockets of local practice and ways of working that does not reflect a consistent approach across the landscape of industries. Ultimately, for some organizations faced with major change, it can be difficult to know which person the sponsor should pick up the phone and contact first—the change or the project manager. Each are able to extol the benefits of their respective disciplines and approaches to the problem in preference to the other, leaving the sponsor uncertain as to the best approach to start the initiative.

6.3   Actualities of Change and Project Management Integration

> **Key Points for Practitioners**
>
> - The project and change management bodies of knowledge have not formalized the key interfaces or integration elements between each of the disciplines; project managers must fully understand the process and scope of the change management requirement to bridge this gap.
> - The resources allocated to the project that are aligned to separate change and project streams must keep focus on the key principle that success depends on an integrated approach.
> - The cultural and political aspects of an organization cannot be ignored when planning the approach to integrating the change and project elements.

Cicmil et al. (2006) proposed a framework for the conceptualization of project actuality by drawing on the insights and discussions from the RPM literature. Cicmil et al. (2006) positioned the RPM approach as one that presents new insights into project management and how it is practiced in real project environments, countering much of the project management literature that does not satisfactorily explain the richness of what actually occurs in project environments. It is this actuality perspective that needs to drive the potential integration of change and project management, not the definition of numerous theoretical frameworks and models that take no account of how practitioners deliver projects and change.

Any proposals for the closer integration of the disciplines must take account of the project and change maturity within organizations and be able to flex and tailor its processes to suit the situation on the ground. Organizations contemplating major transformation projects within a culture not used to change, or have a heavily unionized workforce with a history of resistance, would need to invest in structured approach to managing change that goes beyond the basic stakeholder communication guidance in the PMBoK®. Likewise, change ready organizations used to a culture of project delivery and changing processes and capabilities are not likely to require teams of change management consultants assisting them with resistance mitigation strategies and full implementation of a set of substantial change management processes.

The presented basic themes of closer integration can be classified into a number of overall categories of proposition, each having their benefits and drawbacks. Any practical solution is likely to require a negotiated compromise between all major project and change stakeholders to have a realistic proposition of success. This list is not meant to be exhaustive, but a starting point for further analysis and academic debate.

- *Absorb change management within project management*—this option would have the net effect of creating a single unifying standard for the delivery of projects. Aside from the obvious practitioner governing body political implications, this option would require a step change in the emphasis and approach to the management of projects from a technical oriented delivery perspective to a more people centric, adoption model of success. Research has highlighted that the current skillset valued in project managers is perhaps quite different to the skills and approach needed to deliver change within organizations (Cicmil et al. 2006; Crawford and Hassner-Nahmias 2010). The literature is not clear on whether these skills gaps can be bridged with appropriate training or there is need of a fundamental reassessment of the attributes and experience of people who would be appointed to an integrated role. The simple argument to be articulated in justification of this option could be a focus on an assessment of the set of elements needed to be in place for the delivery and adoption of a successful project, and an appreciation of the benefits in sourcing an approach from a single body of knowledge and standard.

- *Formalize an integration interface* — the current position of unclear separation points and overlaps between the bodies of knowledge and standards from each discipline means that it is unclear on where one starts and the other finishes. An agreed interface between the separate bodies of knowledge (PMBoK® and CMBoK) and various standards that formally recognizes the other discipline could simplify the change and project manager roles and provide clarity to executives. This would require an adoption of agreed terminology in certain areas and a definition of key handover points.
- *Create a new genre that encompasses both disciplines* — a new genre could elevate the emotive debate from *is it a project or change* argument to one that concentrates on successful outcomes irrespective of the road traveled. Equal weight could be given to each of the standards in the form of a unified methodology with an underpinning of distinct body of knowledge.
- *Reconfigure the change and project reporting structure* — this option is perhaps a reaction to the separate change and management reporting structures within organizations where the change team may report to a different set of stakeholders than the project team or competes for resources with the project. This changed structure would include an integrated delivery authority responsible for change and project management that directly reports to the executive.
- *Do nothing* — the *do nothing option* is presented here as an option, but in reality it is likely to be limited by time. It is highly probable that as each of the disciplines updates its separate standards and bodies of knowledge, they will seek to bridge the gaps between the disciplines from the iterations of stakeholder and practitioner feedback. The net effect of this could be an unstructured merging of disciplines that could have negative consequences for organizations wishing to embark on major projects.

The success measures for change and project management should be very closely aligned if not identical. Organizations ultimately wish to utilize an approach that addresses the required technical deliverables but also address the critical people-orientated, cultural, and adoption issues that can significantly affect project success. Establishing a more integrated approach to change and project management could legitimize and standardize the current practices of variable approaches to change that are influenced by an organization's maturity in this area. Executives would need to rely on the experience and expertise of change and project integration practitioners to fully assess the maturity of an organization wishing to embark on a change project. The key task at this early stage would be to identify if the organization is receptive to change and if the executive has experience of working within a project-based structure. The output of this activity would be a recommendation to adapt the activities and resources in support of the project or change activities to fit the organization and the delivery of the successful project. The selected methodology to facilitate this integrated approach would need to be tailored to reflect the organizations' maturity and ability to embrace both change and project activities.

Recommendations for Future Research

1. Closer integration of the change and project disciplines and the analysis of the many and varied complexities and practicalities involved has not seen significant focus from academics (Söderlund (2011)). Further research to identify suitable models and frameworks of an integrated approach is needed.
2. Any closer integration of change and project management needs to balance the *technical* and *people* aspects effectively to deliver the project benefits. The risk of an overemphasis in user participation is the underemphasis of the system and quality aspects (DeLone and McLean 1992). Further academic research is needed to quantify the optimum levels of change and project effort taking into account the culture of the organization and change maturity.
3. Success viewed from both change and project perspectives in the context of an integrated concept has not featured highly in the academic literature. Further research to assess suitable models would benefit the perspectives of success of a joined-up change and project management approach.

Summary of Key Points

- The convergence of project and change management is necessary to deliver projects that satisfy the needs of stakeholders.
- Project success is heavily influenced by the overall organizational approach to change management.
- The concepts, processes, and underlying methods within project and change management are critical to the success of any project. However, the two disciplines have independent standards organizations, routes to practitioner status, and bodies of knowledge, with minimal tangible reference between the two.

(continued)

- In practice rather than project and change management complementing each other, the two disciplines can end up competing over budgets, roles and responsibilities, access to project sponsors, strategy, and execution.
- For some organizations faced with major change, it is not straightforward as to whom the sponsor should contact first—the change or the project manager. Each can potentially highlight the benefits of their respective disciplines and approaches leading to confusion and uncertainty.
- Establishing a more integrated approach to change and project management could legitimize and standardize the current variable approaches to change that are influenced by the maturity of the organizations in this area.

Chapter 7
Conclusion

This book was written to provide a comprehensive text on the subject of IS project success and failure taking account of some of the actualities of project and change management. The key areas of the available literature have been analyzed and discussed where relevant. There are numerous studies exploring this subject, with many attempting to provide frameworks and models to aid our understanding of the key concepts and underlying causes. However, studies have shown that organizations are still more likely to fail to deliver large IS projects than succeed and that smaller projects although not subject to the high failure rates of large ones still have an unacceptable failure rate. Many studies have addressed these issues by attempting to highlight the main causes of failure and by defining the key CSFs that projects need to align with. The acceptance within the industry of the role of stakeholders in project delivery has resulted in a drive for a greater appreciation of their needs and an understanding of their fears of change. The net effect of this has been a rise in the significance of change management as a discipline in its own right and a key component in successful delivery. However, the actuality perspective of how the two disciplines work together has not been widely researched and current practice may leave them both competing for resource and justifying their optimum start point in the project lifecycle. Advocating the closer integration of change and project management has been the theoretical proposition of a small number of studies, but to date the practical real-world perspective on how this is to be actioned has not featured in the literature. The development of an integrated approach that can reduce subjectivity and confusion from managers while delivering a consistent approach; needs to be progressed and formalized to better assure the successful delivery of benefits and to guarantee greater levels of adoption.

© The Author(s) 2016
D.L. Hughes et al., *Success and Failure of IS/IT Projects*,
SpringerBriefs in Information Systems, DOI 10.1007/978-3-319-23000-9_7

Acronyms

ACMP	Association of change management professionals
ADKAR®	Awareness, desire, knowledge, ability, reinforcement
APM	Association for project management
APMG	Accrediting professional managers globally
BoK	Body of knowledge
CMBoK	Change management body of knowledge
CMI	Change Management Institute
CSF	Critical success factor
DMI	Digital media initiative
DSDM	Dynamic systems development method
EIS	Executive information system
ERP	Enterprise resource planning
HISS	Hospital information support system
HIT	Health information technology
IS	Information system
IT	Information technology
LASCAD	London Ambulance Service Computer Aided Dispatch
NAO	National Audit Office
NASA	National Aeronautics and Space Administration
OGC	Office of Government Commerce
PFI	Private Finance Initiative
PMI	Project management institute
PMBoK®	Project management body of knowledge
PMPA	Project management performance assessment
PRINCE2®	PRojects IN Controlled Environments
ROI	Return on investment
RPM	Rethinking project management

© The Author(s) 2016
D.L. Hughes et al., *Success and Failure of IS/IT Projects*,
SpringerBriefs in Information Systems, DOI 10.1007/978-3-319-23000-9

Authors' Bios

Yogesh K. Dwivedi
Professor of Digital and Social Media
Head of Management and Systems Section
Swansea University Bay Campus
School of Management
Fabian Way, Crymlyn Burrows
SWANSEA, SA1 8EN
Wales, UK
Email: ykdwivedi@gmail.com; y.k.dwivedi@swansea.ac.uk

Professor Yogesh K. Dwivedi is a Professor of Digital and Social Media and Head of Management and Systems Section in the School of Management at Swansea University, UK. He obtained his Ph.D. and M.Sc. in Information Systems from Brunel University, UK. He has coauthored several papers which have appeared in international refereed journals such as CACM, DATA BASE, EJIS, IJPR, ISJ, ISF, JCIS, JIT, JORS, TMR, and IMDS. He is Associate Editor of *European Journal of Marketing*, *European Journal of Information Systems*, and *Government Information Quarterly*, Assistant Editor of JEIM and TGPPP, Senior Editor of JECR, and member of the editorial board/review board of several journals.

D. Laurie Hughes
Ph.D. Candidate
Swansea University Bay Campus
School of Management
Fabian Way, Crymlyn Burrows
SWANSEA, SA1 8EN
Wales, UK
Email: 515702@swansea.ac.uk

D. Laurie Hughes is a Ph.D. candidate at the School of Management, Swansea University, UK. He has a B.Eng. in Computer Systems Engineering and an M.Sc.

© The Author(s) 2016
D.L. Hughes et al., *Success and Failure of IS/IT Projects*,
SpringerBriefs in Information Systems, DOI 10.1007/978-3-319-23000-9

(distinction) in Future Interaction Technologies. He has worked as a senior practitioner within UK-based consultancies for a wide range of government and private sector organizations. He has extensive experience in the management of technology-based projects and major areas of transformation.

Nripendra P. Rana
Lecturer of Information Systems
Swansea University Bay Campus
School of Management
Fabian Way, Crymlyn Burrows
SWANSEA, SA1 8EN
Wales, UK
Email: N.P.Rana@swansea.ac.uk

Dr. Nripendra P. Rana is a Lecturer at the School of Management of Swansea University in the UK. He holds a B.Sc., an M.C.A., an M.Tech., and an M.Phil. from Indian universities. He obtained his M.B.A. (distinction) and Ph.D. from Swansea University, UK. He is currently working in the area of technology and e-government adoption. He has varied work experience of teaching in the area of computer engineering and applications at undergraduate and postgraduate levels. He also possesses a good experience in the field of software development. He is a life member of computer society of India.

Antonis C. Simintiras
Professor of Marketing
Gulf University for Science & Technology
Mubarak Alabdullah Area
West Mishref
Block 5
Building 1
Office N1-016
Email: simintiras.a@gust.edu.kw

Professor Antonis C. Simintiras is a Professor of Marketing at Gulf University for Science & Technology. He obtained a BSc (Econ) from University of Macedonia—Greece, an M.B.A. from University of West Haven—USA and a Ph.D. in Sales Management from the University of Huddersfield—UK. Over the years, he has held visiting professorial appointments in various EU states, the USA, and China and published several refereed articles. Part of his work has appeared, among others, in JIBS, IMR, JBR, IMM, P&M, EJM, and JMM. He has contributed to several edited books and coauthored a book on Global Sales Management.

References

Al-Ahmad W, Al-Fagih K (2009) A taxonomy of an IT project failure: root causes. Int Manag Rev 5(1):93–104

Alexander I (1998) Charting a path to project success. Comput Bull 40(4):26

Aslam MB, Asghar S (2008) Inadequate stakeholders involvement in software requirements specification and their impact on is projects success. In: International conference on enterprise information systems and web technologies 2008, EISWT, Orlando, FL, pp 28–32

Ash C (2007) Convergence of it project management and change management: a comparative study. In: Proceedings of the European and Mediterranean conference on information systems, EMCIS 2007, Valencia, Spain, pp 1–8

Atkinson R (1999) Project management: cost, time and quality, two best guesses and a phenomenon, its time to accept other success criteria. Int J Proj Manag 17(6):337–342

Attarzadeh I, Ow, SH (2008) Project management practices: the criteria for success or failure. In: Communications of the IBIMA, vol 1, pp 234–241

Avison D, Wilson D (2002) IT failure and the collapse of One.Tel. In: Proceedings of the IFIP 17th world computer congress – TC8 stream on information systems: the e-Business challenge, pp 31–46

Avots I (1969) Why does project management fail? Calif Manag Rev 12(1):77–82

Baccarini D (1996) The concept of project complexity—a review. Int J Proj Manag 14(4):201–204

Baccarini D (1999) The logical framework method for defining project success. Proj Manag Inst 30(4):25–30

Bannerman PL, Thorogood A (2011) Celebrating IT projects success: a multi-domain analysis. In: Proceedings of the annual Hawaii international conference on system sciences (HICSS), pp 4874–4883

Baker BN, Murphy DC, Fischer D (1983) Factors affecting project success. In: Cleland DI, King WR (eds) Project management handbook. Van Nostrand Reinhold, New York, NY, pp 902–919

Barker T, Frolick M (2003) ERP implementation failure a case study. Inf Syst Manage 20:43–49

Bartis E, Mitev N (2008) A multiple narrative approach to information systems failure: a successful system that failed. In: Proceedings of the 15th European conference on information systems, San Francisco, pp 1421–1433

BBC (2014) BBC was 'complacent' over failed £100m IT project. http://www.bbc.co.uk. Accessed on 19 Sept 2014

© The Author(s) 2016
D.L. Hughes et al., *Success and Failure of IS/IT Projects*,
SpringerBriefs in Information Systems, DOI 10.1007/978-3-319-23000-9

Beckhard RF, Harris RT (1987) Organizational transitions: managing complex change. Addison-Wesley, Reading, MA

Belassi W, Tukel OI (1996) A new framework for determining critical success/failure factors in projects. Int J Proj Manag 14(3):141–151

Beldi A, Cheffi W, Dey P (2010) Managing customer relationship management projects: the case of a large French telecommunications company. Int J Proj Manag 28(4):339–351

Beynon-Davies P (1995) Information systems "failure": the case of the London Ambulance services Computer Aided Despatch project. Eur J Inf Syst 4(3):171–184

Boddy D, Macbeth D (2000) Prescriptions for managing change: a survey of their effects in projects to implement collaborative working between organisations. Int J Proj Manag 18(5):297–306

Breese R (2012) Benefits realisation management: panacea or false dawn? Int J Proj Manag 30(3):341–351

Bridges W (1991) Managing transitions. Perseus, Reading, MA

Bronte-Stuart M (2009) Risk estimation from technology project failure. In: 4th European conference on management of technology, Glasgow, Sept 2009

Brown A, Jones M (1998) Doomed to failure: narratives of inevitability and conspiracy in a failed IS project. Organ Stud 19(1):73–88

Bryde DJ (2003) Modelling project management performance. Int J Qual Reliab Manag 20(2):229–254

Bryde D (2008) Perceptions of the impact of project sponsorship practices on project success. Int J Proj Manag 26(8):800–809

Bryde DJ, Robinson L (2005) Client versus contractor perspectives on project success criteria. Int J Proj Manag 23(8):622–629

Bullock RJ, Batten D (1985) It's just a phase we're going through. Group Org Stud 10:383–412

Buchanan D, Fitzgerald L, Ketley D, Gollop R, Jones JL, Lamont SS, Neath A, Whitby E (2005) No going back: a review of the literature on sustaining organizational change. Int J Manag Rev 7(3):189–205

Burnes B (2005) Complexity theories and organizational change. Int J Manag Rev 7(2):73–90

Bussen W, Myers M (1997) Executive information system failure: a New Zealand case study. J Inf Technol 12(2):145–153

Cable J (2009) An ounce of prevention: a few common-sense measures can go a long way toward preventing IT project failures. Ind Week 258(11):50–51

Cameron E, Green M (2012) Making sense of change management, 3rd edn. Kogan Page, London

Carnall CA (1990) Managing change in organizations. Prentice Hall, London

Change Management Institute (2013) The effective change manager: the change management body of knowledge (CMBoK). VIVID, Sydney

Cicmil SJK, Williams T, Thomas JL, Hodgson DE (2006) Rethinking project management: researching the actuality of projects. Int J Proj Manag 24(8):675–686

Clarke A (1999) A practical use of key success factors to improve the effectiveness of project management. Int J Proj Manag 17(3):139–145

Conboy K (2010) Project failure en mass: a study of loose budgetary control in ISD projects. Eur J Inf Syst 8(40):1–14

Conway CM, Limayem M (2011) "You want it when?" How temporal dissonance in IT workers contributes to project failures. In: International conference on information systems 2011, Shanghai

Cooke-Davies T (2002) The 'real' success factors on projects. Int J Proj Manag 20(3):185–190

Coombs C (2015) When planned IS/IT project benefits are not realized: a study of inhibitors and facilitators to benefits realization. Int J Proj Manag 33(2):363–379

Cowan-Sahadath K (2010) Business transformation: leadership, integration and innovation – a case study. Int J Proj Manag 28(4):395–404

Crawford L (2005) Senior management perceptions of project management competence. Int J Proj Manag 23(1):7–16

Crawford L, Hassner-Nahmias AH (2010) Competencies for managing change. Int J Proj Manag 28(4):405–412

Crawford L, Costello K, Pollack J, Bentley L (2003) Managing soft change projects in the public sector. Int J Proj Manag 21(6):443–448

Creasy T, Anantatmula VS (2013) From every direction – how personality traits and dimensions of project managers can conceptually affect project success. Proj Manag J 44(6):36–51

Cule P, Schmidt R, Lyytinen K, Keil M (2000) Strategies for heading off IS project failure. Inf Syst Manag 17(2):65–73

Davis GB, Lee AS, Nickles KR, Chatterjee S, Hartung R, Wu Y (1992) Diagnosis of an information system failure. A framework and interpretive process. Inf Manag 23(5):293–318

Davis K (2014) Different stakeholder groups and their perceptions of project success. Int J Proj Manag 32(2):189–201

De Bakker K, Boonstra A, Wortmann H (2010) Does risk management contribute to IT project success? A meta-analysis of empirical evidence. Int J Proj Manag 28(5):493–503

Dekkers C, Forselius P (2007) Increase ICT project success with concrete scope management. In: EUROMICRO 2007 – Proceedings of the 33rd EUROMICRO conference on software engineering and advanced applications SEAA 2007, Lübeck, pp 385–392

DeLone WJ, McLean ER (1992) Information systems success: the quest for the dependent variable. Inf Syst Res 3(1):60–95

DeLone WJ, McLean ER (2003) The DeLone and McLean model of information systems success: a ten-year update. J Manag Inf Syst 19(4):9–30

de Wit A (1988) Measurement of project success. Int J Proj Manag 6(3):164–170

Doyle M, Claydon D, Buchanan D (2000) Mixed results, lousy process: the management experience of organizational change. Br J Manag 11:S59–S80

Dwivedi YK, Henriksen HZ, Wastell D, De' RM (2013a) Preface. In: Dwivedi YK et al (eds) Grand successes and failures in IT. Public and private sectors. Springer, Berlin, pp 5–9

Dwivedi YK, Ravichandran K, Williams MD, Miller S, Lal B, Antony GV, Kartik M (2013b) IS/IT project failures: a review of the extant literature for deriving a taxonomy of failure factors. In: Dwivedi YK et al (eds) Grand successes and failures in IT. Public and private sectors. Springer, Berlin, pp 73–88

Dwivedi YK, Wastell D, Henriksen HZ (2015a) Guest editorial: grand successes and failures in IT: private and public sectors. Inf Syst Front 17(1):11–14

Dwivedi YK, Wastell D, Laumer S, Henriksen HZ, Myers MD, Bunker D, Elbanna A, Ravishankar MN, Srivastava SC (2015b) Research on information systems failures and successes: status update and future directions. Inf Syst Front 17(1):143–157

Elkington P, Smallman C (2002) Managing project risks: a case study from the utilities sector. Int J Proj Manag 20(1):49–57

El Emam K, Koru A (2008) A replicated survey of IT software project failures. Softw IEEE 25:84–90

Esa M, Samad Z (2014) Preparing project managers to achieve project success-human related factor. Int J Res Manag Technol 4(2):104–110

Ewusi-Mensah K (2003) Software development failures: anatomy of abandoned projects. The MIT Press, Cambridge, pp 45–64

Ewusi-Mensah K, Przasnyski Z (1995) Learning from abandoned information systems development projects. J Inf Technol 10:3–14

Fenech K, De Raffaele C (2013) Overcoming ICT project failures – a practical perspective. World Congress on Computer and Information Technology, Sousse

Fiedler S (2010) Managing resistance in an organizational transformation: a case study from a mobile operator company. Int J Proj Manag 28(4):370–383

Fisk A, Berente N, Lyytinen K (2010) Boundary spanning competencies and information system development project success. In: ICIS 2010 proceedings – 31st international conference on information systems, Saint Louis, MO

Fitzgerald G, Russo NR (2005) The turnaround of the London ambulance service computer-aided dispatch system (LASCAD). Eur J Inf Syst 14(3):244–257

Flowers S (1997) Information systems failure: identifying the critical failure factors. Fail Lessons Learn Inf Technol Manag 1(1):19–29

Fortune J, White D (2006) Framing of project critical success factors by systems model. Int J Proj Manag 24(1):53–65

Gareis R (2010) Changes of organizations by projects. Int J Proj Manag 28(4):314–327

Gareis R, Huemann M (2008) Change management and projects. Int J Proj Manag 26(8):771–772

Gauld R (2007) Public sector information system failures: lessons from a New Zealand hospital organization. Gov Inf Q 24:102–114

Gibson C (2004) IT enabled business change: an approach to understanding and managing risk. MIS Q Exec 2(2):75–84

Glass RL (2005) IT failure rates – 70 percent or 10–15 percent? IEEE Softw 22(3):110–112

Goulielmos M (2005) Applying the organizational failure diagnosis model to the study of information systems failure. Disaster Prev Manag 14(3):362–377

Gray RJ (2001) Organizational climate and project success. Int J Proj Manag 19(2):103–109

Gustavsson T, Hallin A (2014) Rethinking dichotomization: a critical perspective on the use of "hard" and "soft" in project management research. Int J Proj Manag 32(4):568–577

Heeks R (2002) Information systems and developing countries: failure, success, and local improvisations. Inf Soc 18(2):101–112

Heeks R (2006) Health information systems: failure, success and improvisation. Int J Informatics 75(2):125–137

Hirschheim R, Newman M (1988) Information systems and user resistance: theory and practice. Comput J 31(5):398–408

Hiatt JM, Creasey TM (2012) Change management – the people side of change. Prosci, Loveland, CO

Holland P, Light B, Gibson N (1999) A critical success factors model for enterprise resource planning implementation. In: Proceedings of the 7th European conference on information systems, vol 1, pp 273–297

Hornstein H (2015) The integration of project management and organizational change management is now a necessity. Int J Proj Manag 33(2):291–298

Howsawi E, Eager D (2014) The four-level project success framework: application and assessment. Org Proj 1(1):1–15

Hyvari I (2006) Success of projects in different organizational conditions. Proj Manag J 37(4):31–42

Ika L (2009) Project success as a topic in project management journals. Proj Manag J 40(4):6–19

Jarocki TL (2011) The next evolution – enhancing and unifying project and change management: the emergence one method for total project success. Brown and Williams, Princeton, NJ

Jones C (2004) Software project management practices: failure versus success. J Def Softw Eng 17:5–9

Jones C (2006) Social and technical reasons for software project failures. J Def Softw Eng 19(6):4–9

Jugdev K, Müller R (2005) Retrospective look at our evolving understanding of project success. Proj Manag J 36(4):19

Kappelman L, McKeeman R, Zhang L (2006) Early warning signs of project failure: the dominant dozen. Inf Syst Manag Fall:31–36

Keider S (1974) Why projects fail. Datamation 20(12):53–55

Keil M, Cule P, Lyytinen K, Schmidt R (1998) A framework for identifying software project risks. Commun ACM 41(11):76–83

Kearns GS (2007) How the internal environment impacts information systems project success: an investigation of exploitative and explorative firms. J Comput Inf Syst 48(1):63–75

Kenny J (2003) Effective project management for strategic innovation and change in an organizational context. Proj Manag J 34(2):43–53

Kerzner H (1987) In search of excellence in project management. J Syst Manag 38(2):30–40

Kerzner H (1998) Project management: a systems approach to planning, scheduling and control-ling. Van Nostrad Reinhold, New York

Kerzner H (2013) Project management. A systems approach to planning, scheduling and control-ling, 5th edn. Wiley, Hoboken, NJ

Klaus T, Blanton JE (2010) User resistance determinants and the psychological contract in enter-prise system implementations. Eur J Inf Syst 19(6):625–636

Kliem R, Ludin I (1992) The people side of project management. Gower, Hants

Kloppenborg TJ, Opfer WA (2002) The current state of project management research: trends, inter-pretations and predictions. Proj Manag J 33(2):5–18

Kotter JP (1995) Leading change: why transformation efforts fail. Harv Bus Rev 73(2):59–67

Kübler-Ross E (1973) On death and dying. Routledge, London

Lechler TG, Dvir D (2010) An alternative taxonomy of project management structures: linking project management structures and project success. IEEE Trans Eng Manag 57(2):198–210

Lehmann V (2010) Connecting changes to projects using a historical perspective: towards some new canvases for researchers. Int J Proj Manag 28(4):328–338

Lehtonen P, Martinsuo M (2009) Integrating the change program with the parent organization. Int J Proj Manag 27(2):154–165

Lehtinen TOA, Mäntylä MV, Vanhanen J, Itkonen J, Lassenius C (2014) Perceived causes of soft-ware project failures – an analysis of their relationships. Inf Softw Technol 56(6):623–643

Lemon WF, Liebowitz J, Burn J, Hackney R (2002) Information systems project failure: a com-parative study of two countries. J Glob Inf Manag 10(2):28–39

Lewin K (1951) Field theory in social science. Harper and Row, New York

Leyland M, Hunter D, Dietrich J (2009) Integrating change management into clinical health infor-mation technology project practice. In: World congress on privacy, security, trust and the man-agement of e-business, pp. 89–99

Lin YM, Pan X (2011) Study on risk scenarios of project failure based on Monte-Carlo simulation. In: IEEE 18th international conference on industrial engineering and engineering management, IE & EM, Changchun, pp 1291–1295

Linberg KR (1999) Software developer perceptions about software project failure: a case study. J Syst Softw 49(2):177–192

Lucas H (1975) Why information systems fail. University Press, Columbia, NY

Luecke R (2003) Managing change and transition. Harvard Business School Publishing, Boston, MA

Lyytinen K, Hirschheim R (1987) Information systems failures: a survey and classification of the empirical literature. Oxf Surv Inf Technol 4(1):257–309

Lyytinen K, Robey D (1999) Learning failure in information systems development. Inf Syst J 9(2):85–101

Marnewick C (2012) A longitudinal analysis of ICT project success. In: ACM international confer-ence proceeding series, SAICSIT, SA, pp 326–334

McGrath K (2002) The golden circle: a way of arguing and acting about technology in the London ambulance service. Eur J Inf Syst 11(4):251–266

Michie S, West M (2004) Managing people and performance: an evidence based framework applied to health service organizations. Int J Manag Rev 5(2):91–111

Milosevic D, Patanakul P (2005) Standardized project management may increase development projects success. Int J Proj Manag 23(3):181–192

Mir F, Pinnington A (2014) Exploring the value of project management: linking project manage-ment performance and project success. Int J Proj Manag 32(2):202–217

Mitev NN (1996) More than a failure? The computerized reservation systems at French Railways. Inf Technol People 9(4):8–19

Moran JW, Brightman BK (2000) Leading organizational change. J Work Learn 12(2):66–74

Morris PW, Hough G (1987) The anatomy of major projects: a study of the reality of project man-agement. Major Projects Association, Oxford

Müller R, Turner JR (2007) Matching the project manager's leadership style to project type. Int J Proj Manag 25(1):21–32

Müller R, Judgev K (2012) Critical success factors in projects: Pinto, Slevin and Prescott – the elucidation of project success. Int J Manag Proj Bus 5(4):757–775

Nah F, Lau J, Kuang J (2001) Critical factors for successful implementation of enterprise systems. Bus Process Manag J 7(3):285–296

Nasir MHN, Sahibuddin S (2011) Critical success factors for software projects: a comparative study. Sci Res Essays 6(10):2174–2186

Nawi HSA, Rahman AA, Ibrahim O (2011) Government's ICT project failure factors: a revisit. In: International conference on research and innovation in information systems, Kuala Lumpur, pp 1–6

Nelson R (2007) IT project management: infamous failures, classic mistakes and best practices. MIS Q Exec 6(2):67–78

Newman M, Sabherwal R (1996) Determinants of commitment to information systems development: a longitudinal investigation. MIS Q 20:23–54

Nixon P, Harrington M, Parker D (2012) Leadership performance is significant to project success or failure: a critical analysis. Int J Product Perform Manag 61(2):204–216

O'Connor M, Reinsborough L (1992) Quality projects in the 1990s: a review of past projects and future trends. Int J Proj Manag 10(2):107–114

Oakland J, Tanner S (2007) Successful change management. Total Qual Manag Bus Excell 18(1–2):1–19

OGC Group (2013) Managing successful projects with PRINCE2. TSO, London

Oreg S (2003) Resistance to change: developing an individual differences measure. J Appl Psychol 88(4):587–604

Oreg S (2006) Personality, context, and resistance to organizational change. Eur J Work Org Psychol 15(1):73–101

Pan G, Hackney R, Pan SL (2008) Information systems implementation failure: insights from prism. Int J Inf Manag 28(4):259–269

Papke-Shields KE, Beise C, Quan J (2010) Do project managers practice what they preach, and does it matter to project success? Int J Proj Manag 28(7):650–662

Park CW, Keil M, Kim JW (2009) The effect of IT failure impact and personal morality on IT project reporting behavior. IEEE Trans Eng Manag 56(1):45–60

Parker D, Charlton J, Ribeiro A, Pathak RD (2013) Integration of project-based management and change management – intervention methodology. Int J Product Perform Manag 62(5):534–544

Partington D (1996) The project management of organizational change. Int J Proj Manag 14(1):13–21

Patton N, Shechet A (2007) Wisdom for building the project manager/project sponsor relationship: partnership for project success. J Def Eng 20(11):4–9

Perkins TK (2006) Knowledge: the core problem of project failure. J Def Eng 19(6):13–15

Pettigrew AM, Ferlie E, McKee L (1992) Shaping strategic change: making change in large organizations – the case of the national health service. Sage, London

Pettigrew A, Whipp R (1993) Managing change for competitive success. Black, Oxford, pp 269–295

Philip T, Schwabe G, Ewusi-Mensah K (2009) Critical issues of offshore software development project failures. In: Proceedings – 30th international conference on information systems, ICIS 2009, Phoenix, AZ

Pinto JK, Mantel SJ (1990) The causes of project failure. IEEE Trans Eng Manag 37(4):269–276

Pinto JK, Slevin DP (1987) Critical factors in successful project implementation. IEEE Trans Eng Manag 34(1):22–27

Pinto JK, Slevin DP (1988) Project success: definitions and measurement techniques. Proj Manag J 19(1):67–72

Pinto JK, Prescott J (1988) Variations in critical success factors over the stages in the project life cycle. J Manag 14(1):5–18

Poulymenakou A, Holmes A (1996) A contingency framework for the investigation of information systems failure. Eur J Inf Syst 5(1):34–46

Procaccino JD, Verner JM, Shelfer KM, Gefen D (2005) What do software practitioners really think about project success: an exploratory study. J Syst Softw 78(2):194–203

Project Management Institute (2014) A guide to the project management body of knowledge (PMBOK® guide), 5th edn. PMI, Newtown Square, PA

Prosci (2012) Best practices in change management. Prosci benchmarking report. Prosci®, Loveland, CO

Purvis R, Zagenczyk T, McCray G (2015) What's in it for me? Using expectancy theory and climate to explain stakeholder participation, its direction and intensity. Int J Proj Manag 33(1):3–14

Qureshi TM, Warraich AS, Hijazi ST (2009) Significance of project management performance assessment (PMPA) model. Int J Proj Manag 27(4):378–388

Rana NP, Dwivedi YK, Williams MD, Weerakkody V (2015a) Investigating success of an e-government initiative: validation of an integrated IS success model. Inf Syst Front 17:127–142

Rana NP, Dwivedi YK, Williams MD, Lal B (2015b) Examining the success of the online public grievance redressal systems: an extension of the IS success model. Inf Syst Manag 32(1):39–59

Rana NP, Dwivedi YK, Williams MD (2013) Evaluating the validity of IS success models for E-Government research: an empirical test and integrated model. Int J Electron Gov Res 9(3):1–22

Rob M (2003) Project failures in small companies. IEEE Softw 20(6):94–95

Rogers EM (1962) Diffusion of innovations. Free Press, Glencoe

Sauer C (1993) Why information systems fail: a case study approach. Alfred Waller, Oxford

Sauer C, Southon G, Dampney C (1997) Fit, failure, and the house of horrors: toward a configurational theory of IS project failure. In: Proceedings of the 18th international conference on information systems, ICIS, Atlanta, pp 349–366

Sauser J, Reilly RR, Shenhar AJ (2009) Why projects fail? How contingency theory can provide new insights – a comparative analysis of NASA's mars climate orbiter loss. Int J Proj Manag 27(7):665–679

Schein E (1992) Organizational culture and leadership, 2nd edn. Jossey-Bass, San Francisco, CA

Shenhar A, Dvir D, Levy O, Maltz A (2001) Project success: a multidimensional strategic concept. Long Range Plan 34(2001):699–725

Schmidt R, Lyytinen K, Keil M, Cule P (2001) Identifying software project risks: an international Delphi study. J Manag Inf Syst 17(4):5–36

Scott J, Vessey I (2000) Implementing enterprise resource planning systems: the role of learning from failure. Inf Syst Front 2(2):213–232

Senge P, Kelner A, Roberts C, Ross R, Roth G, Smth B (1999) The dance of change. Nicholas Brealey, London

Shanks G, Parr A, Hu B (2000) Differences in critical success factors in ERP systems implementation in Australia and China: a cultural analysis. ECIS, Vienna

Sitkin SB (1992) Learning through failure: the strategy of small losses. Res Organ Behav 14:231–266

Söderlund J (2004) Building theories of project management: past research, questions for the future. Int J Proj Manag 22(3):183–191

Söderlund J (2011) Pluralism in project management: navigating the crossroads of specialization and fragmentation. Int J Manag Rev 13(2):153–176

Standing C, Guilfoyle A, Lin C, Love PED (2006) The attribution of success and failure in IT projects. Ind Manag Data Syst 106(8):1148–1165

Standish Group (2013) CHAOS manifesto think big act small. Boston. Retrieved from http://www. standishgroup.com. Accessed May 2015

Stanley D, Meyer J, Topolnytsky L (2005) Employee cynicism and resistance to organizational change. J Bus Psychol 19(4):429–459

Stummer M, Zuchi D (2010) Developing roles in change processes – a case study from a public sector organization. Int J Proj Manag 28(4):384–394

Sumner M (1999) Critical success factors in enterprise wide information management systems projects. In: Proceedings of the 1999 ACM SIGCPR conference on computer personnel research, pp. 297–303

Sumner M, Bock D, Giamartino G (2006) Exploring the linkage between the characteristics of it project leaders and project success. Inf Syst Manag 23(4):43–49

Toney F, Powers R (1997) Best practices of project management groups in large functional organizations. Proj Manag J 33

Tukel OI, Rom WO (1998) Analysis of the characteristics of projects in diverse industries. J Oper Manag 16(1):43–61

Turner JR (2009) The handbook of project-based management: leading strategic change in organizations, 3rd edn. McGraw-Hill, London

Turner J, Müller R (2005) The project manager's leadership style as a success factor on projects: a literature review. Proj Manag J 36(2):49–61

Umble EJ, Haft RR, Umble MM (2003) Enterprise resource planning: implementation procedures and critical success factors. Eur J Oper Res 146(2):241–257

Verner JM, Abdullah LM (2012) Exploratory case study research: outsourced project failure. Inf Softw Technol 54(8):866–886

Verner J, Sampson J, Cerpa N (2008) What factors lead to software project failure? In: Proceedings of the 2nd international conference on research challenges in information science, RCIS 2008, Marrakech, Morocco, pp 71–79

Voropajev V (1998) Change management—a key integrative function of PM in transition economies. Int J Proj Manag 16(1):15–19

Wallace L, Keil M, Rai A (2004) Understanding software project risk: a cluster analysis. Inf Manag 42(1):115–125

Ward J, Elvin R (1999) A new framework for managing IT-enabled business change. Inf Syst J 9(3):197–221

Warne L, Hart D (1997) Organizational politics and project failure: a case study of a large public sector project. Fail Lessons Learn Inf Technol Manag 1(1):57–65

Wateridge J (1995) IT projects: a basis for success. Int J Proj Manag 13(3):169–172

Wateridge J (1998) How can IS/IT projects be measured for success? Int J Proj Manag 16(1):59–63

White D, Fortune J (2002) Current practice in project management – an empirical study. Int J Proj Manag 20(1):1–11

Winch G, Meunier M-C, Head J, Russ K (2012) Projects as the content and process of change: the case of the health and safety laboratory. Int J Proj Manag 30(2):141–152

Winklhofer H (2001) Organizational change as a contributing factor to IS failure. In: Proceedings of the Hawaii international conference on system sciences, Hawaii

Winter M, Smith C, Morris P, Cicmil S (2006a) Directions for future research in project management: the main findings of a UK government-funded research network. Int J Proj Manag 24(8):650–662

Winter M, Smith C, Cooke-Davies T, Cicmil S (2006b) The importance of 'process' in rethinking project management: the story of a UK government – funded research network. Int J Proj Manag 24(8):638–649

Wirth I, Tryloff D (1995) Preliminary comparison of six efforts to document the project-management body of knowledge. Int J Proj Manag 13(2):109–118

Yeo KT (2002) Critical failure factors in information system projects. Int J Proj Manag 20(3):241–246

Young R (2005) An example of relevant IS research for top managers on IT project failure. In: Proceedings – 16th Australasian conference on information systems, ACIS 2005. Sydney, pp 14

Index

© The Author(s) 2016
D.L. Hughes et al., *Success and Failure of IS/IT Projects*,
SpringerBriefs in Information Systems, DOI 10.1007/978-3-319-23000-9

Printed in the United States
by Bookmasters

Printed in the United States
By Bookmasters